The *Journey* of MY LIFE:

A Chronological Review of Events Throughout My years

ALBERT C. WIGGINS III

INTRODUCTION

A wise man or woman will understand the philosophy of increased education and it's benefits. The fear of the Lord's requirements is the beginning of knowledge. Some despise institutions because of its formalities the heart to learning is reprobation, rejection to the process to make the imagination or memory repugnant.

Prove all things that matter on your way to success.

Prove all things and hold fast to that which is good. Note: A gracious woman retained honor in strong men.

I wrote this book, not so much about myself, but of events throughout the years. A chronological snapshot of events during my years of existence. The events as I display in this book – historical events – it is obvious that history repeats itself. I also include international crisis and newsworthy events from various news sources. In addition, I wanted to highlight historical figures throughout those many years that are and were impressive during my lifetime.

I am in awe at what Black folks have accomplished over the years. Amazing. I have lived to 85 years, living longer than both my parents, plus my only sibling. This book covers years from my birth up to 2020.

Without the help of my wife, Dorothy Wiggins, this book would not be a reality. I cannot type a lick, so she took on the task of typing and helping with some editing.

If I can say one thing about all these years of life, I can truthfully say that I am blessed and thankful to live a good life. So, put on your seatbelt while we ride the ups and downs on this journey called life!!!!

BIOGRAPHICAL NOTE

I WAS BORN July 24, 1936 and, became involved with practical duties around the age of 10, although often interrupted I was persuaded to resume work. I was by chance just seized upon what others have, so I decided more than an impulse, to not have my life forced to dwell and conceal my being just in a dream, by clinging to a higher power. The courage I just unveiled to myself by faith and constant trust.

Inside the gate of love with clutching hands and a friendly light, a glow of Mephistopheles for knowledge and power..I surrounded myself with shared intellects for a pathway to success.

CHAPTER 1

Godly principals will give you a direction that repenting is a philosophy of asking for forgiveness so now I feel my spirit cleansed.

THE YEAR 1936

In July 1936 I was born and had no convections, no direction or no idea if I was a girl or a boy – like all infants who are totally dependent on your mother's nurturing care.

In this same year that I was born, Adolf Hitler opened the 11th Olympic Games in Berlin, Germany.

Jesse Owens was a Gold Medal winner. He won Gold for 100 Meters, win a gold medal for 200 Meters and won 4 x 100 Meter Race.

Owen's, in the long jump his Olympic records equaled 4 world records.

His return to the United States was racially denied recognitions by President Roosevelt.

Owens ended his athletic career shortly after the 1936 Olympics.

In 1936, I was born in the Boston City Hospital July 24th. Raised by a mother only because my father left before I really had a chance to know him. My Mom taught me to respect other, especially women. We were poor, but I did not know it because everyone we knew in the neighborhood were in the same situation; at least we had food on the table each day.

At the age of 18, I joined the Airforce and while there served as a medic in the hospital emergency room plus played football for 13th Airforce.

After serving four years in the USAF, I signed up for electronic school through the Veterans Administration. It took two years to complete.

In 1958 I married a wonderful girl that gave me three healthy children. In my late sixties, my wife of many years passed away which was in 2002.

In the year 2004 I remarried to a ravishing lady named Dorothy. By the way, this was my mother's name! The meaning of the name, Dorothy, means "A Gift of God", which she is.

Going back to the time I was in the Air Force; I did a bad thing in my life while overseas. I fathered a child name Elizabeth. I deserted my responsibility as a dad when she was only two months old. But through the grace of God, she found me in the United States over four years ago through Facebook. I am extremely happy she has forgiven me for not being there for her as a father.

CHAPTER 2

The YEAR 1938

This is the year I was 2 years old and was unaware of what was going on in the world, but it was moving quickly.

- Major news stories included:
- The first use of a seeing eye dog.
- Minimum hourly wages were .25 cents an hour.
- Seabiscuit beats War Admiral – the horse race of the year.
- Oil is discovered in Saudi Arabia.
- Germany begins persecution of Jews.
- Howard Hughes sets a record by flying around the world in 3 days and 19 hours.
- In Europe, Germany was planning its strategy of war.
- On September 21st, a hurricane slammed into Long Island with little or no warning from the weather service. The hurricane caused 40-foot waves to hit Long Island and sixty-three thousand people were left homeless and some 700 dead.
- Max Schmeling was defeated by a knockout in the 1st round by Joe Louis (The Brown Bomber) for the Heavyweight Championship.

The Fair Stand Labor action created several important things:

- It defined the maximum work week as forty-four hours in a seven-day week.

- It created a national minimum wage.
- It made employers pay employed time and a half for overtime.
- It also stopped oppressive child labor in most cases.

Now I'm only 2 years old, and way too young to figure things out.

Note the development of a child's personality has been studied in many ways. Some of its results is scored by the income of our parents, and the type of education that eventually insert you into the rank of the middle class.

CHAPTER 3
Years 1939 – 1949

In the year 1939 and creativity at three years old was a nurture controversy, playing with my younger brother, Frederick. Attitudes and values were not a consideration with Fred and I, and current events was not part of our discussion. It was about playing and eating.

The Year 1940

It was a Leap Year; 940th year of the 2nd millennium and 40th year of the 20th Century and the 1st year of the 1940's.

- WWII the Soviet 44th rifle division is destroyed by Finnish Forces.
- British submarine HMS Starfish is sunk
- WWII Winter War – Soviet Forces launch a major assault on Finnis troops occupying the Karelian Isthmus.

Albert Wiggins is 4 years old, and my personality development has changed somewhat. My mother is talking to me about school and my socializing skills. Socializing skills has been a cultural conditioning approach (I must have read that statement somewhere).

The Year 1941

The events of WWII:

- January-August 10,072 men, women and children with mental and physical disabilities are asphyxiated with carbon monoxide in a gas chamber at Hadamard euthanasia center in Nazi Germany in the first phase of mass killings under the action T4 program here.
- Franklin D. Roosevelt is sworn in for a third term as President of the United States.

The Year 1942

Now, Albert Wiggins is 5 years old, between the age 4 and 5 the child developed a sense of initiative in this stage. There is a conflict between his natural strivings and his development. I'm learning inner controls based on the teaching of my mother Dorothy Wiggins. It's called a butt whooping! But at this age you count on your mom for everything.

Major Event in Boston, Ma.

- Coconut Grove fire in Boston. The Coconut Grove Fire was a night club fire in the United States. It was a premier night club during the post prohibition 1930's and 1940's in Boston. November 28, 1942, it was the scene of the deadliest night club fires in history killing 492 people which was 32 more than the building authorized capacity and injuring hundreds more. The scale of the tragedy shocked the nation and briefly replaced the events of World War II in newspaper headlines. It led to reform of safety standards and building codes across the United States and major changes in the treatment and rehabilitation of burn victims internationally.

This fire was the second-deadliest single building fire in American history, only the 1903 Lroguois Threater fire in Chicago had a higher death toll of 602.

Seventy-five years later, Coconut Grove Fire still haunts the fire department in Boston. Stanley Tomaszewski, a 16-year-old busboy was blamed by many for starting the blaze.

Victims and Escapees:

1. Well known movie-cowboy actor – Buck Jones.
2. Scott R. Dunlap was hosting a party. He survived.
3. Band Leader, Musical Director, Bernice Fazioli lost his life.
4. Bandleader Mickey Albert escaped out of the basement window.

The location of Coconut Grove Club was Bay Village, Boston.

The Year 1943

Now I'm 7 years old and trying to earn recognition by producing things. Things like drawings in school, making up my bed, trying to wash dishes by standing on a chair to complete the task. Back in those days you could go to the neighborhood movies for .10 cents if you were 13 and younger.

Notable Events 1943:

Negro League star Josh Gibson suffers a nervous breakdown.

Canadian Army troops arrive in North Africa.

William H. Hastie, civilian aide to secretary of War, resign to protest segregation the in the Armed Forces.

The first United States President to visit a foreign country in war time. FDR leaves for Casablanca, Morocco.

WWII Franklin D. Roosevelt travels from Miami to Morocco to meet with Winston Churchill becoming the first American President to do so.

First transport of Jews from Amsterdam to concentration camp Hertogenbosh Vugh located near the Netherlands.

Duke Ellington plays at Carnegie Hall in New York City for the very first time.

The Year 1944

I am now 8 years old in the 4th grade and starting to notice cultural limitations in my grammar school which was 90% white students. Therefore, history lessons were primarily focused on accomplishments of the white majority. I was never taught in school about black inventors, scientists or politicians. What I only learned of black history was about slavery.

My life was disrupted when I had to attend a school for slow learners which was stacked with all black children. These students were labeled as having cultural limitations, learning disabilities and the confusion about our identity was noticed in all of the students. We could not date, for one, we were too young or because the neighbors knew if you went to the George T. Angel School you were clarified as a dummy.

A couple or more years later, I was transferred to the 7th grade in a regular junior high school. Perhaps it was the results of a test that was given to me at the request of one of my teachers who saw more in me and what I could accomplish. That test proved; I had no learning disabilities.

The Year 1944

Great things happening during this year:

- First feature-length foreign movie was shown.
- African Journey shown on T.V. NYC.
- The first use of a helicopter during warfare (British Atlantic Patrol).
- Ralph Bunche appointed 1st Negro official in the U.S. State Department.
- U.S. Air Force announces production of 1st U.S. Jet Fighter – The Bell P-59
- The Metropolitan Opera House in New York City hosts a Jazz Concert for the first time. The performers were Louis Armstrong, Benny Goodman, Lionel Hampton, Artie Show, Roy Eldridge and Jack Teagarden.

The Year 1945

- In the month of February my second wife, Dorothy, was born in a little town in Newton, North Carolina.
- The United Nation was born and each of the 193 member states of the United Nations is a member of the general assembly states and are admitted to membership in the UN by a decision of the General Assembly upon the recommendation of the Security Council.

The UN's Responsibility:

1. Maintain international peace and security.
2. Protect human right.
3. Deliver Humanitarian aid.
4. Promote sustainable development.
5. Uphold international law.

The Year 1946

Things of interest during this year:

1. Cher – born Cherilyn Sarkisian on May 20th. She was often referred to as the Goddess of Pop.
2. ENIAL, U.S. 1st computer finished by Mauchly/Eckert.
3. Vietnam holds its first ever general election.
4. U.S. Army established 1st radar contact with the moon, from Belmar, New Jersey.
5. January 22 – U.S. President Harry Truman sets up the Central Intelligence Agency (CIA).
6. Ted Williams is offered $500,000 to play in the Mexican Baseball League. He refuses.
7. Jack Robison debuts as 2nd baseman for the Montreal Royals.

8. Red Sox win 15th straight games. Beats Yankees 5-4. DiMaggio hits a grand slam.

Now I'm 10 years old and in my neighborhood going to George Tangell School was a curse. It had no academic freedom to pursue and teach relevant knowledge without restrictions. To be favorably accepted in my poor community it was all about scholastic abilities. As time passed by, I taught myself not to be the definition of unintelligence by reading whatever books I could get my hands on as if the world were watching. In the 1940's was available always was discarded newspapers.

The Year 1947

Here are a few things that happened during this time:

1. Mahatma Gandhi begins march for peace in East Bengal. He was a pacifist and spiritual leader.
2. William Dawson becomes 1st Black to head the Congressional Committee.
3. Toronto Maple Leaf rookie Howie Meeker scores 5 goals in a game.
4. Small river steamer sank on Yangtze River. Kills 400.
5. 1st Black reporter in U.S. congressional press gallery (Peneival Prallis).
6. Mahatma Gandhi begins his final fast.

Now, I'm 11 years old and I still think of personality and intelligence as an aspect of personality because it is controlled by factors that affect others and has been observed to enhanced by a number of factors, nutrition and health, self-image and motivational conditioning. This is not a conclusion I came up at this young age, but throughout my life, especially after attending college (later on in the book).

The Year 1948

Events of this year:

1. Gandhi was assassinated in New Delhi by a Hindu Militant on January 30th.

2. Communists seize power in Czechoslovakia February 23-25 during this year.

3. President Harry Truman urges Congress to adopt a Civil Rights Program.

4. 1st Lt. Nancy Leftenant becomes first Black in Army Nursing Corps.

5. During May of this year, the independent Jewish State of Israel was created in Palestine by the United Nations. The creation of Israel marked the first time in 2000 years that an Independent Jewish State had existed. David Ben Gurion became the newly formed country's first Prime Minister.

6. The National Party of the Dutch Afrikaners begins the polity of apartheid in South Africa.

Now I'm just 12 years old and during this time in my life, the important thing was sports. Sports gave me a sense of belonging. I started playing Catholic Youth Organization baseball (CYO). Sports in these days was a popular activity for me and a lot of youth. I felt special to be able to go to Fenway Park and Braves Field to see the Boston Braves (Now Red Sox) play.

I remember how poor we were in these days. My mother worked as a domestic, cleaning houses of wealthy whites. My contribution was by shining shoes in downtown Boston and selling newspapers. I always managed to give my mother half of my earnings. The other half went to baseball games to see the Boston Braves play. Back then the price of a ticket in the bleachers was fifty cents.

The street where we lived everyone in our neighborhood were poor. But you know, all the kids in the area did not really know this. In the end, something magical happened, since we all survived to become accomplished adults.

The Year 1949

After the misery of living through the depression and World War II, companies are now able to supply cars and supply televisions. Some 6.2 million new cars sold in the United States.

Television Programs appears which we now call Soap Operas.

Cost of Living in 1949:

- Cost of a new home - $7,450.
- Average wage per year - $2,950.
- The cost of a gallon of gas was .17 cents.
- Cost of a new car was $1,420.
- Minimum hourly wage – .70 cents per hour.
- Coffee was .85 cents for a 2lb bag

In this same year, The Soviet Union created its first Atomic Bomb, Color T.V. was made by RCA and the Polaroid Camera was produced and sold for $89.95.

CHAPTER 4
Years 1950-1959

The Year 1950

Now I am 14 years old, handsome – if I say so myself – but still no girlfriend. All my boys had at least experienced sex, but I remained a virgin because I was too busy playing sports, especially CYO baseball (Catholic Youth Organization). Before joining, I asked one of my friends from school how I could join the team. He said, "You have to be a Catholic to play." Okay, so I became Catholic…took catechism classes and lo and behold, became a Catholic! This opened the door for me to join the hardball youth group.

America has the largest Police Association in the World with almost 420,000 members. The International Police Association is an independent body of members of the police service, whether on active duty or retired.

The Year 1951

Things of Interest:

1. "Life After Tomorrow" was the first film to receive an X rating.
2. Boxing Title Fight: January 12 Ezzard Charles won by technical knockout (TKO) over Lee Oma in 10 rounds for the heavyweight boxing title.
3. China refuses cease fire in Korea.

4. U.S. performs nuclear test at Nevada Test Site.

5. Largest purse to date in horse racing was $144,323, won by Great Circle.

6. St. Louis Browns sign on pitcher Satchel Paige (Black baseball player)

7. Kwame Nkrumah wins 1st Parliamentary election in the Gold Coast (Ghana).

8. February 14, Sugar Ray Robinson defeats Jake LaMotte and takes the Middle-weight title.

9. Twenty-Second (22nd) amendment ratified, limiting U.S. Presidents to two 4-year terms.

10. U.S. soldiers in Korea numbered 2,900,000.

Now that I am 15 years old, I thought to myself, "No more vacillating. I'll stay focused to where my intellect will take me at this state of the game."

While at the George T. Angel School, a White man came to evaluate students. After my reading test, he said I was too intelligent to be located at this institution and placed me into the regular school system. This made me happy, and I was hoping by this time I could get a girlfriend. Reality took me down a different avenue, tenuous is the right word. My thoughts were that when I become older, the experience will cause my intelligence to be a major move into an exceptional pastoral acceptance. It was a thought.

The Year 1952

1. The Today Show premiers on NBC becoming one of the longest-running television series in America.

2. In the U.S. a mechanical heart is used for the first time in the human patient.

3. Emmett Ashford becomes the first African American umpire in organized baseball by being authorized to be a substitute.

4. The U.S. Senate ratified a peace treaty with Japan.

5. The crash of the U.S. Airforce C124 Globe Master at Moser Lake Washington kills 86 servicemen.

6. Nearly 58,000 cases of Polio are reported in the U.S. Three thousand one hundred and forty-five (3,145) die and twenty-one thousand two hundred and sixty-nine (21,269) are left with mild to disabling paralysis.

Now, I'm 16 years old, fantasizing about girls, thinking about sports, work and school. "Things happen for a reason" and my reason, "I'm sure these things would materialize soon." I listen to my contemporaries' stories how successful in these relationships with girls…some even call out names.

I continue to play sports and was called a "lame", but I laughed it off, but I was okay with it.

Maybe a 16 year older have tendencies to be surreptitiously about 23 the facts.

During this time there was a selection of different Boy's Club members to work on the sidelines at the Boston Garden in Massachusetts. I was chosen, out of the four kids, to retrieve professional basketballs when it went off the side of the court, which was an exciting experience. To top it off, I was thrilled to see Bob Cozy's basketball skills. He played guard for the Boston Celtics from 1950 to 1963 and was voted into 13 NBA all-star games.

As I mentioned earlier, my entire neighborhood I grew up in was poor. Along the way I've come across many different types of people…black and white… saints and corrupted. I remember knowing Steve Fleming and Whitey Bulger, who became notorious gangsters as reported. Although he was a little older than me, Stevie, (his nickname) seemed like the nicest White boy that I knew back in those days. I was surprised as I grew into an adult that he was a hitman for Whitey.

I also had the privilege of knowing the infamous Reverend Michael Haynes, Pastor of 12th Baptist Church in Roxbury. He lectured and mentored over 400 kids in every attempt to keep them on the right track in building self-esteem and preparing them for college. Then there was Bootsy Ramsey (Alfreda

Ramsey). A long-serving Boston school committee member, who founded the SAT Preparation Program serving high school students in Boston, while also founding and coordinating girls' basketball leagues and Amateur Athletic Union teams for the city. She also founded the Owen Wells Fitness Center and the Reebok Educational Athletic Partnership that provides students with community programs in social development, computer skills and tutoring. Someone to truly be admired.

Whatever Rev. Haynes did for the boys in our neighborhood, Bootsy did as much for girls.

My most admiration was for my mother. She worked so hard to keep food on the table and clothes on our back. I also considered her an assassin; By that, I mean she did not spare the rod in keeping me and my brother on the straight and narrow. She would pick up anything close to her to whack us into oblivion.

This timeframe was a blur, but I remember seeing the Pope (don't remember which one) on the Boston Commons. By this time in my life, I had a lot of friends, Black and White. God was exceptionally good to me. He put me in an area where the teachers and parents were articulate.

The Year 1953

I mentioned earlier that my aunt Peggy was extremely ill with Tuberculosis and was admitted into a long-term care facility. My Mom moved Aunt Peggy's two girls (my cousins) into our home to care for them while her sister was isolated until healed. Now our family grew from three members to five. Feeling that it was a little crowded in our home, I decided to quit school and go into the military. The first action taken was applying for the Air Force at the downtown Boston Commons' office. The officer on duty explained to me that I needed my mother's signature due to fact I was not eighteen years of age.

When I presented the application to my mother, she immediately refused to sign. Maybe she thought I was too young to enter the military or that I was helping with bringing in a couple of dollars to the family expenses on my part-time pay. So much for going into the service!!

Some Interesting information I came across:

Thirty-five dialogues and thirteen letters [the Epistles] have traditionally been ascribed to Plato, thought modern scholars doubt the authenticity of at least some of these Plato's writings have been published in several fashions, this has led to several conventions regarding the name and referencing of Plato's tests.

Narration of the dialogues Plato never presents himself as a participant in any of the dialogues, and except for the apology is among the most frequently read of his works in the apology, Socrates tries to dismiss rumors that he is a sophist and defends himself against charges of disbelief in the gods and corruption of the young. Well, that is enough of ambiguous.

Sometimes in life, as you age, your philosophy becomes cloudy and whenever interpretations can become inundated and we may not realize that it has taken place.

The Year 1954

Now, Albert is 18 years old and felt liberated enough to make decisions on my own. I dropped out of high school and joined the United States Air Force.

Suddenly I had three pair of shoes with no holes in them and was provided four full-dress military outfits. This was more clothes I have ever had in my life.

The next step I was being sent to New York for basic training and from there to Rapid City, South Dakota for six months. I thought Boston was cold, but whew, this was the coldest place that I have ever witnessed. The military taught me how the medical system works and trained me as an emergency room technician.

The military had a program in place whereas you send money home, and they would match 40%. I did not make much but was able to set up a monthly payment for my mother of $50; and the Air Force matched it with $40. My mother received $90.00 monthly for the four years I spent in active duty. We were so poor, this amount went a long way in helping out, especially with extra mouths to feed.

My philosophy as a man, you cannot do enough for your mother or a wife because they bring life into this world. I think women are one of God's greatest creations.

The Year 1955

Events of this year!

1. Panamanian President Jose Antonio Ramon is assassinated.
2. Marian Anderson becomes the 1st African American to perform with the New York Metropolitan Opera.
3. U.S. and Panama sign anal treaty.
4. First Presidential news conference on Network TV, Dwight Eisenhower gave.
5. Israel acquires 4 to 7 Dead Sea Scrolls.
6. Elvis Presley makes his 1st TV appearance on a broadcast of radio show "Louisiana Hayride".

The Year 1956

Albert Wiggins is leaving Rapid City, South Dakota after six months of training in the medical field. On my way to the Philippine Islands what I read about is that it has 7,000 islands in the Western Pacific Ocean. The islands entail 114,830 square miles with a population of 40,000,000.

The military ship transporting us to the islands was inundated with military personnel, but what really fascinated me was the blue color of the ocean. You see when I was a child in the first grade, my teacher would say during art, "Now class, color the ocean blue and green." I had no idea what she was talking about, because the ocean I played in at City Point, South Boston was brown.

Only until then while sailing to the Philippines that I realized the ocean is truly blue and green.

Continuing our odyssey, stopping in Kwajalein, Guam located in the Mars Hall Island American Naval Base and then to the Philippines and Clark Air Force Base. Once we got settled, there was a two-week restriction period for orientation reasons. We learned all the do's and don'ts of mingling with the local ladies. In the Philippines there were some of the most ravishing women in the world. I was not sure how I was going to handle women due to the fact; I am a 19-year-old virgin.

As time passes, I became cognitive about women and concluded that by studying and interacting with women I figured out that they were fun to be around and truthful. If they like you – they will display that to you and if they did not like you…well, they will let you know that very quickly. As time passes, I became more comfortable around the ladies, and my desires were more relaxed.

This same year, I try out for the football team and made first string for 13th Air Force as a wide receiver for offense and defense. I played 15 games of football and we never lost a game. It was a thrill to hear 500 military men shouting my name whenever the coach took me out of the game. WIGGINS, WIGGINS!!!!! That experience will always be with me.

Another experience while in the military, but not so pleasurable, was a plane crash. I was a trained emergency medic, and my job was to care for injured people on the base. One day the emergency phone rang, and the location of the call was at the airbase. It was for a plane crash. When I got into the back of the ambulance on our way to the airport, the grassy area was burning and near that area was a dead pilot. Part of his arms and legs were gone. I had to pick him up and place his remains in a body bag. The condition of his body was shocking, but I remain stoic even to this day. I remember clearly how devastating it was and to this day cannot release that picture out of my mind. I even have nightmares.

Serving my country in the USAF continue from 1954 to 1958. Although I loved serving my county, some of the military's policy was esoteric. The good stuff came in many ways, like seeing Hong Kong for the first time in 1956. There were 5 Air Force buddies who toured in this area with me. We almost starved to death because we could not read the menu and there were no interpreters to help. It was educational going from the Hong Kong side to Calhan side, shopping, flirting with the ladies and enjoyed our stay at the hotel. Other experiences like working with the money exchange and riding the man driven taxi called the Calera. The exception was the Chinese people who were gracious to all of us Black soldiers from the United States.

Happenings during this year:

1. 1956 the increase in living standards
2. College education was 1 in 3 high school graduates going to college.
3. The movie The Ten Commandments was made.
4. U.S.A. Rocky Marciano retires as the only undefeated Heavy Weight Champion of the world with a perfect record.
5. The first computer hard drive invented by IBM.
6. Alabama bus segregation law declared illegal by the U.S. Supreme Court.
7. U.S. President Dwight D. Eisenhower signs into law 1956 Federal-aid Highway Act, the interstate system with the construction of over 41,000 miles. The cost estimated at $25 to $30 billion.
8. Grace Kelly married Prince rainier.
9. Eight Black students are refused entry at Sturgis High School in Sturgis, Kentucky.
10. Oral vaccine developed against Polio by Albert Sabin.

I am still in the Philippine Islands and through my observations the true Filipino was my color, "dark brown", and their size and height were maximum

4 feet tall. The United States government provided them free medical care because of their assistance is killing so many Japanese during the Second World War. The complexion of the so-called Negredo to this day is the same. The light-skinned Filipinos are a mixture of Asian and Spanish.

The Year 1957

What happened in 1957...glad you asked!

1. It was the peak of the baby boomer years.

2. Asian Flu pandemic claims over 150,000 lives.

3. Future astronaut, John Glenn sets the transcontinental speed record from Los Angeles to New York three hours and twenty-three minutes.

4. Hurricane Audrey hits the United States' Gulf Coast killing about 500 people.

5. During September of this year, nine African American students enrolled at Little Rock Central High School in Arkansas, all White school. They were met with distain.

I left the Philippines going to Wright Patterson Air Force Base in Dayton, Ohio. Delighted to be back in the interior (U.S.), the first thing I did was to check out the football facilities. There was not one. The A.F. replacement officer did not tell the truth in the details. The closest to the game I loved was touch football. It is not the same as tackle, like the game played in the Philippines.

While in the Philippines, I fathered a child with one of local women. I gave this child her name, Elizabeth. I have regretted several things in life, but this action is on the top of the list. I abandoned this baby!

In Ohio, I had a lot of fun and met some nice people, especially women. One was a nurse and an officer. I was truly lucky not to get caught in our relationship. It could have cost both of us our military positions. My obligation to the military was up in one year, so I was incredibly careful in my mannerism and not to screw up. Having an honorable discharge would help my goals become a reality... I could to school on the veteran's plan.

The Year 1958

I was released from the Air Force in the year 1958 with an honorable discharge. I did not want to continue in the medical field but that was all I knew. I had no choice. Therefore, I ended up working at the Veterans Administration Hospital in Boston. It lasted about six months. I asked to be on a permanent night shift, and they refused my request. Okay, so I gave my resignation and ended up working at the University Hospital, Boston, on the night shift taking care of quadriplegics and paraplegic patients.

The Year 1959

I was pretty much on my way to goals set. I developed this indomitable attitude too soon because of my over confidence. I forgot you had to put in sleep time and homework. But the road to my goals would not be defeated by excuses.

This was the year I got married to my first wife, Betty after a short engagement. Before marriage, I did mention that I had fathered a child in the Philippines and needed her help in locating her. I did not have much money, but that was nothing new. My respect for the U.S. Air Force was no longer an assumption of its help for me and my future, it was seminal. So much for organizational experience. The average yearly wages in those days, was $5,000-$6,000. We had a small amount coming from USAF and another small amount coming from my wife's job at AT&T. My night job was less than my day, but we got by.

My plan was to be accepted by the Industrial Technical School for Electronics. I graduated and went to work with a company called Transitron in Wakefield, Massachusetts.

Happenings during this year:

1. Fidel Castro comes to power.
2. Alaska becomes the 49th State of the U.S.
3. USSR – The Luna 2 Spacecraft crashes into the moon.
4. Hawaii becomes the 50th State of the U.S.
5. U.S. unemployment reaches 1.4 million.
6. Typhoon Vera with winds over 160 MPH strikes Japanese Island of Honshu killing nearly 5,000 people.
7. The first known human with HIV dies in the Congo.

The Year 1960

What happened to me in 1960 was psychologically justifiable to benefit me. After my marriage to a lovely woman, we were starting a family which produced 3 incredible children. In 1961 Stephanie became our 1st creation. In 1962, along came Gregory and finally in l964 Valerie was born.

I graduated from the Industrial Technical School in Boston with a certificate in electronics. I applied for a job that same week and was hired. Unfortunately, the job lasted only three years when the renunciation of the contract fell through. What hurt me most of all, was the relationship built around work friends which was severed after leaving the job.

Things of Interest:

1. John F. Kennedy announces his candidacy for the U.S. Presidency.
2. John Reynolds set age of solar system at 4,950,000,000.
3. Elvis Presley goes into the Army.
4. U.S. and Japan sign joint defense treaty.
5. Rock falls traps 437 at Colebrook, South Africa – 417 die of methane poisoning.
6. High School basketball sensation, Danny Heater, scores 135 points.

7. Four students stage 1st civil rights sit-in at Woolworth's lunch counter in Greensboro, N.C.

8. Boston Celtic, Bill Russell, becomes 1st NBAer with 50 rebounds.

9. Jimi Hendrix, rock and Roll Guitarist, plays his first gig.

10. Wilt Chamberlain sets NBA playoff record of 53 points.

11. Sharpeville Massacre, police kill 72 in south African and Outlaw the ANC.

12. Pope John appoints the first Japanese, African and Filipino cardinals.

CHAPTER 5

(The Years 1961-1970)

The Year 1961

Things of Interest:

1. Barack Obama was born in 1961.

2. Birth of Hip Hop is now a multi-billion-dollar industry.

3. Racial riots at the University of Georgia

4. President Dwight Eisenhower allegedly orders assassination of Congo's Lumumba.

5. J.F. Kennedy is inaugurated as President of the United States.

6. Lazard Brothers Ltd. draw a check for $334,867,807.68.

7. Boston Celtic Bill Russell grabs 40 rebounds to beat Golden State Warriors 136-125.

8. Frank Sinatra launches Reprise label under Warner Bros. Records.

9. Floyd Patterson K.O.'s Ingmar Johansson in 6 rounds for heavyweight boxing title.

10. After a 4 ½ year trial, Nelson Mandela is acquitted of treason in Pretoria.

11. Barbara Streisand appears on the Jack Paar TV Show.

The Year 1962

Now, Albert is 26 years old with a 24-year-old wife 2 and ½ kids working two jobs falling asleep everyplace I sat. My wife was a stay-at-home mother, therefore, I had to bring home the bacon for her to make ends meet. During this time, I'm not quite sure of the exact dates, but a friend introduced me to a contact that knew key folks with the Boston Red Sox. I always prided myself as a pretty good ball player, either in football or baseball. To my surprise, I received a letter providing me with an interview date. I never knew what would have happened if I'd follow through on that interview. After thinking it over about feeding the family and keeping a roof over our heads, I did not follow through. There are not guarantees that one if picked for the Major Leagues, especially during the 60's in Boston…and that I'm Black!! When I shared this story recently, one of my Boston friends asked me, "What was the interview for, janitor?"

Things of Interest:

1. United States Navy Seals established.

2. NFL prohibits grabbing of face masks.

3. Operation Chopper begins – America is first combat mission in the Vietnam War.

4. Wilt Chamberlain of Golden State Warriors scores then NBA record 73 points vs Chicago Bulls.

5. Jackie Roberson is the first American Black elected to Baseball Hall of Fame.

6. James Meredith is the first Black to enroll in the University of Mississippi.

7. The U.S. Supreme Court rules that officially sponsored prayer in public school is unconstitutional.

8. Sonny Liston knocks out Floyd Paterson to win the World Heavyweight Championship.

9. Marilyn Monroe dies of barbiturate overdose at the age of 36.

The Year 1963

This year, I turn 27 years old, working my butt off raising small children and driving a taxi. Plus, I was working full time in the Boston Navy Shipyard in the radar department for AN/SPN 29 and 40 radar systems. I was meeting nice associates and going on sea trials. This job lasted about 8 years, and I looked forward to retiring from the Navy Shipyard, but President Nixon closed a lot of shipyards, Boston included. There must have been 5,000 employees out of work this year.

Things of Interest:

1. George Wallace sworn in as Governor of Alabama. His address states, "segregation now, segregation tomorrow, segregation forever."
2. Jim Thorpe, George Halas, Red Gangs elected to Football Hall of Fame.
3. Willie Mays, San Francisco Giants, signs a record $100,000 per year contract.
4. Bob Cousy plays his last NBA game, March 17, 1963.
5. March 21, Alcatraz prison in San Francisco Bay closes.
6. April 9th, Winston Churchill becomes 1st honorary U.S. Citizen.
7. U.S.S. Thresher, a nuclear-powered submarine sinks 220 miles east of Boston – 129 men, including 17 civilians died.
8. Jews are exiled from Brun Monrovia by order of King Ladislaus.

The Year 1963

Interesting Events:

1. Jan 11th Discotheque opens – Whiskey-A-Go-Go – in Los Angeles.
2. President John F. Kennedy killed in Texas on November 22nd.
3. 1st Class postage stamp raised from .4 cents to .5 cents.
4. Poet Robert Frost wins Bollinger prize.

5. The last prisoners walk down boardwalk as Alcatraz Federal Penitentiary closes.

6. American Airlines DC-10 crashes on takeoff from Chicago, Illinois killing 273 including 2 people on the ground.

7. 95-year old woman scores a hole-in-one in Florida.

8. A train crash in Tanga Mozambique kills 19 people.

The Year 1964
The years are flying by! I am now 28 years old.

Interesting things this year:

1. President Lyndon B. Johnson declares "War on Poverty".

2. Anti-U.S. rioting broke out in Panama Canal Zone.

3. U.S. Surgeon General, Luther Terry reports that smoking maybe hazardous.

4. Jacqueline Kenny's 1st public appearance on television since U.S. President JFK's assassination.

5. The plan for World Trade Center announced.

6. Jeff Bezos founder of Amazon.com born in Albuquerque, New Mexico.

7. Michelle Obama, first African American 1st lady (2009-2016) born in DeYoung, Illinois.

I am beginning to recognize my characteristic abilities. My values could be presented as a pattern change from season to season. With this esoteric pattern change, I must ask myself, "Am I doing enough for myself at this stage of my life?" I think your personality is your "book of life." I think matters are a mental game of hide and seek and is a personality conflict on a road not taken. The best way to vicissitudes is one who constantly writes in his mind, is good for me and my family. Is the philosophy or the pursuit of wisdom by intellectual means and laws underlying reality?

The Year 1965

Events of Interest:

1. January 2, Martin Luther King, Jr. begins a drive to register Black voters.

2. Jan 4, Lyndon B. Johnson's "Great Society" State of the Union address.

3. Winston Churchill at St. Paul's Cathedral in London, England was the largest state funeral.

4. February 1st Martin Luther King, Jr. and 700 demonstrators arrested in Selma, Alabama.

5. Alabama state troopers and 600 Black protestors clash in Selma.

6. First nonstop helicopter crossing North America by JR Wilford.

7. Beatle's "Eight Days A Week" recording single goes #1 and stays number 1 for two weeks.

8. Rolling Stones fined $35 each for public urination.

Albert (Jeepy) Wiggins in 1965 is now 29 years old. I left General Electric two years prior, and the transition was not difficult because of my certification in electronics. The subject matter of electronics versus radar systems are similar. The U.S. government sent me to San Francisco to learn A/San-29 radar system. This position placed me in the pool for sea trials. I did not like being on the ship for 2 or 3 days and away from family.

As I mentioned before, the Boston Navy Shipyard was closed which left a lot of workers, close to retirement, were placed in an inordinate position. Some were transferred to other locations, but not me.

The Year 1966

Things of Interest:

1. All U.S. cigarette packs must carry "caution, cigarette smoking maybe hazardous to your health".

2. 1st Jewish child born in Spain since 1492 expulsion.

3. Floyd B. McKissick, named national director of C.O.R.E. (Congress of Racial Equality.)

4. Georgia House of Representatives votes 184 to 12 to deny Julian Bond his seat as a result of his opposition to the Vietnam War.

5. 550 died in landslide in mountains behind Rio de Janeiro after rainstorm.

6. Red Auerbach wins his 1000th game as coach of NBA Boston Celtics.

7. 1st Black selected for presidential cabinet. LBJ selects Robert C. Weaver – HUD.

8. Martin Luther King Jr. opens campaign in Chicago.

9. Willie Mays signs highest contract $130,000 per year.

10. Wilt Chamberlain breaks NBA career scoring record at 20,884 points.

11. Barbara Streisand stars on "Color Me Barbara" special on CBS.

12. Aug. 5 – Martin Luther King Jr. stoned during Chicago march.

13. Aug. 6 Muhammad Ali Kos Brian London in 3rd round for heavyweight boxing title.

14. Oct. 12th Jimi Hendrix experience performs with Noel Redding and Mitch Mitchell.

15. Bobby Orr debut for the Boston Bruins.

Now I am a happy 30-year-old. If I can remember correctly, I was still working for the U.S government at the Boston Navy Shipyard and it was full time. I loved the job and had the chance to meet some nice friends, especially those I met on the ship as radar technicians who had more experience in radar than me. As I reflect to that time, I do not remember their names; the past is so ambiguous when you try to recall events 50 years prior. I can assert that all my life, God has provided me with three beautiful children and as time moved forward to the present there are two more children added to the credence.

As I reflect on my past parenthetical past, maybe slightly a cut off from the specified numerical times of these events, but nothing is expatiated.

The Year 1967

Events of Interest:

1. Israel defeats Arab forces in a six-day war, which ends with Israel occupying the Sinai Peninsula and other territories.

2. Vietnam War Operation Cedar Falls starts.

3. Segregationist Lester Maddox is sworn in as Governor of Georgia.

4. The N.Y. Times reports that the U.S. Army is conducting secret germ warfare experiments.

5. Albert DeSalvo is convicted of numerous crimes and sentenced to life in prison.

6. In Munich, the trial begins with Wilhelm Harster accused of the murder of 82,856 Jews, including Anne Frank.

7. American researchers discover the Madrid Codices by Leonardo da Vinci in the National Library of Spain.

8. The 25th Amendment to the U.S. Constitution is enacted.

9. Hans Albrecht Bethe, contributor to astrophysics quantum electro-dynamics and solid-state physics won the 1967 Nobel Peace Prize in physics for his work on the Theory of Steller Nucleosyntheses.

10. The U.S. Supreme Court case Loving versus Virginia established the right of Americans to marry whom they wish.

The Year 1968

What was Albert (Jeepy) Wiggins doing currently? One year after graduating from the Navy Radar School which was interesting. I seriously entertained the narrative of events concerning the amount of money that could be made over 20 years employed by the government, which was a satisfying thought.

My electronics skills increased ascensional. As time passed in the world of radar electronics, rumors were casually being predicate, concerning the closing of the Boston Naval Shipyard. I tried to overthrow these rumors, but as time passed by the rumors got louder and louder.

The Charleston Navy Shipyard built, repaired, modernized and resupplied ships for 174 years from Boston ships and the sailors serving aboard set off to places around the globe. The ships that left the Yard represented the United States on every continent and defended the nation through both times of war and peace. The generation of workers at the Yard took pride in the significance of what they contributed and the work that they completed for many sailors this was the last touch of American soil for months, years or perhaps never again.

Operationally the Yard saw many periods of expansion and decline as the policies of the United States changed over the course of two centuries. Technologically, the Yard saw constant transformation and acted as a hub of innovations. When the Yard opened, it serviced wooden sailing ships and employed tradesmen such as carpenters, ropemakers and ship riggers. When the Yard closed in 1974 the Yard had welders, electricians, machinists, iron workers pipefitters and engineers.

<u>Historical Note</u>: **Black men in navy blue**; during the American Civil War Navy yards like Charlestown had to build and out dozens of war ships to help the Union Navy successfully blockade the Confederate States of America. Once off to the sea, the Navy required thousands of men to serve as crewmen aboard the hundreds of ships involved in the blockade. Critical in this effort was the role of African American sailors in the Union Navy in 1863; for example, roughly 20% of all Naval enlistees were African American.

Women workers at the Boston Navy Shipyard during World War I.

In the Spring of 1917, more than 2 years before the 19th Amendment granted women the right to vote, a radical transformation was taking place at the Boston Navy Shipyard. The United States Navy adopted a radical enlistment policy that opened its doors clerical ranks to educated White women parallel to this national watershed, the Boston Navy Shipyard know knows as the Charlestown Navy hired civilian women as unskilled laborers for the first time in history.

Boston Navy Yard and the great war "1914-1918"

At the turn of the 20th Century, the Boston Navy Shipyard, now known as Charlestown Navy Yard, entered its second century of service by embarking on its first major expansion since the Civil War. This push for preparedness grew more intense when World War I began in 1914 when U.S. join the war, the Yard would reach its greatest rate of production yet in history.

"We Can Do It"- Shipbuilding women inside the Charlestown Navy Yard.

The 17,000 civilian employees on the Boston Navy Shipyard's 1941 rolls were not numerous enough for the facility to increase building, converting and repairing ships to levels demand by wartime needs. To get the work done, Boston Navy Shipyard turned to people who normally would not be hired, namely women. By mid-1943 over 50,000 civilians came to work each day at the shops, offices, piers and day docks of the Boston Navy Shipyard. Between 15% and 20% of these workers were women.

The USS Alligator Shipwreck of 1820; At the Charlestown Navy Shipyard in Boston Massachusetts.

It is an excellent example of an American warship from this period, the Alligator accompanied the slave trade off the coast of Africa and protected merchant ships in the West Indies from pirates. These were two of the most significant issues on President James Monroe's agenda. By the time Monroe took office, it was illegal to transport new slaves to the United States from Africa and the United States Navy was called to enforce that law. The Alligator was one of the many ships that patrolled the shores of West Africa to curtail illegal slave trading. The Alligator also transported Dr. Eli Ayres who was a representative of the American Colonization Society. He traveled to Africa to buy land that became a colony for freed African American slaves. This new place formed in 1847 is now the country of Liberia.

The Alligator was also used to combat piracy in the Caribbean which became an issue in 1819. This same year Spain ceded Florida to the United Stated. The United Stated became responsible for protecting merchant ships off the coast of Florida from pirates.

The Alligator met many pirate ships in combat during the Spring and Summer of 1822. In November of this year, it ran aground while escorting a convoy of merchant ships. After unsuccessfully attempting to refloat the vessel, the crew set it on fire to prevent pirates from salvaging the wreck. The Alligator is 86 Feet in length and 25 feet at the beam. The wreck consists of two ballast piles and associate coral heads and rubble. The primary ballast pile consists of the remains of the lower hull, which are preserved on site. The second pile contains artifacts from the vessel, as well as components of the Alligator that were jettisoned overboard when the crew tried to refloat the ship today. The Alligator has stabilized and is in a fair state of preservation.

Today the USS Alligator wreck lies 200 feet southwest of Alligator reef lighthouse, off the Islamorada located in the Florida Keys National Marine Sanctuary. The wreck is submerged in 3.12 feet of water.

The Year 1969

Things of Interest:

1. Australian Rupert Murdock gains control of the News of the World.

2. Lorraine Hansberry's "To be Young Gifted and Black" premiere in New York City.

3. February 4 the Palestine National Congress appoints Yasser Arafat chairman of the Palestine Liberation Organization (PLO).

4. Golda Meir sworn in as the first female Prime Minister of Israel.

5. "Cloud Nine" by the Temptations is released by a duo or group, won Billboard Album of the year 1969.

6. General Hafez Al-Assad becomes head of Syria through a military coup.

7. Men's figure skating championship in Colorado Springs won by Tim Wood USA.

8. April 4, 1969, Haskell Karp receives the first temporary artificial heart, implemented by a surgeon Denton Cooley at Texas Heart Institute in Houston.

9. Student Afro-American Society seized at Columbia College.

10. North Korea shoots at U.S. airplane above Japanese sea.

11. April 17, Sirhan Sirhan is convicted of assassinating U.S. Senator Robert F. Kennedy.

The Year 1970

According to the United Nations, the world population reaches 3.63 billion. Due to behaviors of the world governments a Non-Prolife Nation Nuclear Treaty went into effect, and it was ratified in the United Nations March 1970. The purpose of the treaty was to prevent the further spread and creation of nuclear weapons, to work towards complete disarmament.

My answer to the above statement is to create an agency that have direct dialog and is represented in an agreement with all countries under a United Nation colors. Revolutionized the old psychology and creativity. Talking in the past is not working. Now it is about attitudes with the show of strength. Now is the time that the world to become friends, not just beneficial to the clashes of philosophy of the wealthy but reinforce the idea about becoming a legacy.

Other matters of Interest:

1. Cyclone in Bangladesh kills 500,000.

2. Earthquake in Peru kills 67,000.

3. Environmental Protection Agency (EPA) begins operation in 1970.

4. 100,000 people demonstrate in Washington against the Vietnam War.

5. United States invade Cambodia.

6. U.S. increases import duty taxes to protect American jobs.

7. U.S. lowers the voting age to 18.

8. "No Fault" divorce law in California was established.

9. Average income per year is $9,400.

10. United States postage stamps is .6 cents.

CHAPTER 6
(Years 1971-1980)

Albert (Jeepy) Wiggins in 1971 is 35 years old!! Betty, my wife at this period of my life was working for Trans World Airlines (TWA) at Logan Airport in Boston, Massachusetts. I'm still a full-time employee with the United States government.

It was a congratulatory life I was living, because of my wife's employment. We were able to travel, space available on flights at no cost. We were able to take the children on trips to Disney Land, Disney World and all places of interest because of amenities of TWA.

I remember during this year; cigarette advertisements were banned on television, and I was still smoking. I remember the Globetrotters lost by 1 point to New Jersey Reds. I remember "Sonny" Liston was found dead. I remember Congressional Black Caucus organizers and I also remember The Baseball Association announces a special Hall of Fame Wing for Black players.

Things of Interest
1. Intel releases the world's first microprocessor.
2. Charles Manson and 3 of his followers receive the death penalty.
3. Walt Disney World Resort opens in Florida.
4. In 1971 the average house cost $5,632.

5. This year marked the start of the digital age when the microprocessor was invented.

6. Mariner 9 Spacecraft stopped its communications in 10/72 and is expected to remain in orbit around Mars for 50 years.

7. The New York Times begins to publish sections of the Pentagon Papers starting on June 13th showing the U.S. government had been lying to the American people.

8. China is admitted to the United Nations.

9. A new stock market index called the NASDAQ debuts.

10. Decimalization in United Kingdom and Ireland both switch to decimal current.

11. Tsunami (ocean wave) in the Bay of Bengal in Orissa State in India kills 10,000.

The Year 1972

Things of Interest

1. Policewomen are enlisted as full members of South African Police Force for the first time.

2. Jan 28th, Garfield Todd, former Prime Minister of Southern Rhodesia and his daughter, Judith, supporters of Black majority rule in the country, are arrested.

3. Bootlegger sells wood alcohol to wedding party – 100 died in New Delhi.

4. Jan 30th, Bloody Sunday 27 unarmed civilians are shot (of whom 14 were killed) by British Army during a civil rights march in Derry. This was the highest death toll from a single shooting incident.

5. Aretha Franklin sings at Mahalia Jacksons funeral.

6. 1st scientific hand-held calculator (HP-35) introduced at a price of $395.

7. California Supreme Court abolishes death penalty.

8. March 3, sculpted figures of Jefferson Davis, Robert E. Lee and Stonewall Jackson are completed at Stone Mountain, Georgia.

9. March 9, "The First Time Ever I saw Your Face" single released by Ewan McColl Billboard – number 1 song in 1972, also released by Roberta Flack – Billboard song of the year.

10. March 22nd, Congress approves Equal rights Amendment (never ratified).

I am now 36 years old. Things I remember during this year's news, was the Munich Olympics terrorist attack. Mark Spitz won 7 Gold Medals. This was the year Governor George Wallace is shot.

I started looking at homes and came across a split-level home with living room, dining room, three bedrooms, cathedral ceilings, three baths, central air and double garage on the Cape in Massachusetts. I thought the asking price was too high at $32,400. Can you imagine what it is going for in today's market?

This year was also the beginning of the biggest political scandal in modern times and the start of the Watergate Scandal. The Grand Jury Indicted E. Howard Hunt Jr. and G. Gordon Liddy for conspiracy, burglary and violation of Federal wiretapping laws.

Lastly, during this time, the last U.S. ground troops withdrawn from Vietnam.

The Year 1973

Important News:

1. Average cost of a new house is $32,500.

2. Average income per year is $12,900.

3. Roe versus Wade, Supreme Court of the United Stated rules on this case Jan. 22nd. Roe versus Wade makes abortion a U.S. constitutional right.

4. United States Vice President Agnew resigns, dealing with charges of tax evasion and receiving bribes prior to resignation.

5. U.S. troops withdraw from Vietnam and U.S. involvement in Vietnam, war ends with the signing of peace.

6. Israel shoots down Libyan passenger plane.

7. USA – Sears Tower is completed during May. The 1,729-foot-tall structure became the tallest building in the world, a title that is held for 25 years until the Petronas Towers in Malaysia were completed in 1998.

8. Watergate hearings begin in the United States Senate and President Richard Nixon

9. Tells the nation, "I am not a crook."

10. Yom Kippur War was the fourth and largest Arab-Israeli conflict begins as Egyptian and Syrian forces attack Israel.

The Year 1974

Albert Wiggins is now 38 years old, and the cost-of-living expenses has increased over last year.

I remember the cost of a new house is now $34,900. Average income per year is $13,900 and monthly rent is $185. A dozen of eggs cost 0.45 cents and a gallon of gas is 0.35 cents.

Also, Richard Nixon becomes the first U.S. President forced to resign following impeachment hearings which began May 9th, after the Watergate Scandal.

I also remember the "Rumble in The Jungle" on October 30th. The much-hyped boxing match between George Foreman and Muhammad Ali for Ali to regain his heavyweight boxing title which takes place in Kinshasa, Zaire (Democratic Republic of the Congo).

U.S. President, Gerald Ford gives unconditional pardon to Richard Nixon.

The World population estimate reaches 4 billion people.

The Year 1975

Interest of the Year:

1. Cost of Living: the cost of a gallon of gas is .44 cents.
2. Cost of Living: the average cost of a new card is $4,250.
3. Cost of Living: the housing prices are at $11,787.
4. Cost of Living: a gallon of Petrol is .72 cents.
5. The South Vietnamese President resigned, and South Vietnam surrendered unconditionally to the North. The United States' involvement in the war ended.
6. Major World Political Leaders 1975:

    a. Australia's Prime Minister Gough Witham until 11/November/1975
    b. Brazil's President Emesto Geisel.
    c. Canadian Prime Minister Plere Trudeau.
    d. China's chairman of The People's Republic of China – post abolished.
    e. France's President Valery Giscard D'Estaing.
    f. German chancellor Helmut Schmidt.
    g. India's Prime Minister Indira Gandhi.
    h. Italy's Prime Minister Aldo Moro.
    i. Japan's Prime Minister Takeo Meld.
    j. Mexico's President Luis echeveria.

The Year 1976

Events of the Year:

A cosmopolitan lifestyle of inflation continues to be a problem around the world.

1. China earthquake in Tangshan China on July 28th kills 655,000.

2. Italy's earthquake measuring 6.5 on the Richter scale strikes in Northeastern Italy.

3. Philippines – Tidal Wave in the Philippines kills 5,000.

4. United Kingdom – Worst drought on record hits Britain, forcing the use of standard pipes.

5. Thirty-two Black African Nations boycott Montreal Olympics in protest to continued sporting links between New Zealand and South Africa.

The Year 1977

Events of the Year:

1. Quebec adopts French as the official language.

2. Elvis Presley dies from a heart attack at age 42.

3. New York City blackout lasted for 25 hours and resulted in looting and disorderly conduct.

4. The U.S. returns the Panama Canal back to Panama.

5. United States commodore PET Computer released. The first all-in-one personal computer the Commodore PET was introduced as a prototype at the Consumer Electronic Show during January of 1977. PET stood for "Personal Electronic Transactor" and was the world's first PC to be sold to regular retail consumers. It came equipped with a monitor keyboard and a cassette tape drive that was originally priced at $495. The price increased to 4595 as the product proved to be popular. The original Commodore PET had just 4 kilobytes of memory, but the company soon offered an upgraded model with 8 kilobytes of RAM.

6. Egypt leader President Anwar Al-Sadat breaks rank with other Arab Nations and recognizes the State of Israel.

7. 165 people die in Beverly Hills Supper club fire on May 28th.

8. In July, the first Apple 1 personal computer kit goes on sale for $666.66. January 3rd Apple Computer incorporated by Steve Jobs and Steve Worniak.

9. April 16th the Apple computer was introduced at the first West Coast Computer Fair. On June 5th, the Apple II goes on sale for the base price of $1,298 rising to $2,638 depending on installed memory. The original Apple II tech spec used MOS technology 6502 microprocessors running at 1 MHZ 4KB of RAM at audio cassette interface for loading programs and storing data.

The Year 1978

This is the year I started working at the MBTA (Massachusetts Bay Transportation Authority) until 1999. I spent 21 years of service in the accounting department. Our responsibility was to pay 7,000 weekly and 1,300 by-weekly employees.

During the first year there, I applied and tested for a position as car, or inhouse repairman. Unfortunately. I was refused the position due to my high blood pressure, which I didn't know I had. So, I decided to adjust to being in the treasurer's department and as time passed by, I learned how to be a contributor of importance and was promoted to the executive role. The pay was good, and the benefits were excellent.

When I reflect to those working days, I was reminded that when you achieve your goals, you acknowledge that any effective program would demand full time involvement. It is interesting to note modification is needed for a preview and one need to keep priorities straight.

What made me successful in the accounting department was my gregarious personality, although my intellect was average. I developed a supplication to ask people who were over me in rank, how they got to be in their position of responsibility they currently held. If they liked me, they would tell me.

I wrote a biography of the information that was given to me and some had to be tenuous, of little significance.

The Year 1978

Interesting Things Happening:

1. Richard Chase was an American serial killer who snuffed out six people in the span of a month in Sacramento California. He was named "The Vampire of Sacramento" because he drank his victims' blood and cannibalized their remains.

2. Theodore Robert Bundy (born Theodore Robert Cowell, November 24, 1946.) January 24, 1989 was an American serial killer, kidnapper, rapist, burglar, thief and necrophile who assaulted and murdered numerous young women and girls during the 1970's and possibly earlier. Shortly before his execution and after more than a decade of denials, he confessed to 30 homicides that he committed in seven states between 1974 and 1978. The true number of victims' court will forever be unknown and could be much higher than the number to which Bundy confessed.

3. Tennessee Governor Bill Haslam says he has exonerated a man, Lawrence McKinney, whose conviction for rape and robbery were set aside by a court in 2009 and who was released after more than three decades in prison.

4. Egypt and Israel sign the Camp David Accords to secure peace between the two nations.

5. Gold reaches an all-time high of $200 per ounce.

6. Rhodesia's Prime Minister Ian Smith and three Black leaders agree on the transfer to Black Majority Rule.

7. Serial killer David Berkowitz, the "Son of Sam", is sentenced on June 12th to 25 years to life in prison.

8. The cost of a new house is now at $54,800 in 1978.

I learned from the Bible about Prophecy. With regards to God's Word: Prophets receive and speak the Word of the Lord and so prophetic words have the same destructive and creative power as the Lord's own Words, Jeremiah 1, a prophet declares something to be over, and it is over. He makes something new happen by speaking prophetic speech is performative, such as, "I now pronounce you man and wife" in a prophetic declaration so are, "Here I stand" and "When in the course of human events…"

When our World became Christian. Whether Europeans accept that debatable conclusion or nor, Verne's Slim Volume is an essential antidote to the misinformation about Europe's Christian beginnings, that has become the received Orthodox and for that same reason, it is a gift to American Christians as well.

The Year 1979

Albert (Jeepy) Wiggins is now 43 years old and have noticed the cosmopolitan lifestyle of the most casual observers is silent. I have tried to understand the attitude and psychology of our World Leaders and I have concluded that those who rule our World are not nice people.

I think the majority of the World's citizens would be satisfied with a home, a job and return home to a family. Maybe a congratulatory remark from those who rule. Perhaps the solution might be in one World Government that represents all people, starting with free education, a cultural landscape that all countries can participate in this philosophy. I am sure God did not mean for us to kill each other just because our skin is of a different color. There is a narrative floating out there that nice people of the World have no voice, but that has changed. Over a phase of a few years, most people have figured out what is going on in the World.

Things of Interest:
1. American Airlines Flight 191 crashed and exploded in the field near O'Hare International Airport in Chicago.
2. China institutes the one child per family rule to help control its exploding population.
3. The first Led-Black Government of Rhodesia in 90 years takes power on June 1st and the countries' name is changed to Zimbabwe.

4. Eleven fans are killed, and dozens are injured at a Who concert (a Rock Group) at the Riverfront coliseum in Cincinnati, Ohio.

5. The United States and Soviet Union reach an agreement during the strategic arms limitations talk during June of 1979.

6. Michael Jackson releases his breakthrough album "Off the Wall" on August 10th.

7. In this year, 1979, for the first time in history a woman, Margaret Thatcher, is elected Prime Minister in the United Kingdom.

8. The average house price is $13,650.!!!!

The Year 1980

I am now 44 years old. New technology allows for new consumer products. Along came the first Fox Machines out of Japan. Also, Digital Equipment Corporation, Intel and Xerox introduce the DIX Standard for Ethernet.

CNN began broadcasting on June 1st. The American based network was headquartered in Atlanta, Georgia and founded by Ted turner. It was the first 24-hour news show. The network originally struggled to find success but by mid-1980's it had gained more influence and became well known for its live coverage of events as they happened; often being the first to broadcast during big news events.

Politics enters the Olympic games with a boycott by the United States of the Moscow Olympics.

Other interesting events:

1. Ronald Reagan's election was the most significant news story of 1980.

2. The hostages in Iran had the greatest "headline impact" during this year.

3. United States experience racial unrest.

4. The average cost of new homes reaches $68,700.

5. There was a failed operation by the U.S. to free hostages in Iran.

6. Mariel boat lift mass exodus of political refugees from Cub to the United States.

7. Former Beatles John Lennon is shot to death.

CHAPTER 7
(Years 1981-1990)

I became more and more aware of self, first with thinking more about prophecy, the world's unrest and now Love! Love at first sight is not a myth. It is declared a new life because we all discovered that. We ask, will life be easier or more difficult? The unscripted belief if you have someone to love, the manual for Love has not been written. Webster defines Love as an intense affection for another person. I think that is partly right; only not complete.

The Year 1981

Interesting Events:

1. January 16th Leon Spinks (Boxer) is mugged. His assailants even took his gold teeth.

2. January 19th Muhammad Ali talks a despondent 21-year-old out of committing suicide.

3. January 20th Ronald Reason inaugurated as the 40th President of the United States of America.

4. February 1 Duke Ellington's musical "Sophisticated Ladies", premiers in New York City.

5. February 6, Crime file "fort Apache", the Bronx, starring Paul Newman released amid protests in the U.S.

6. Event of interest, March 1 Duke Ellington's musical "Sophisticated Ladies" opens in Lunt-Fontanne, New York City for 767 performances. He was Jazz musician and composer.

7. March 2, Aircraft hijacked by 3 Pakistani terrorists.

8. March 5th, U.S. government grants Atlanta $1 million to search for Black boy murderer.

9. Daylight Saving Time is introduced in the USSR.

10. April 7th, album release "Street Songs" 5th studio album by Rick James is released – earned Billboard album of the Year).

11. Boxing title fight April 11th Larry Holmes beats Trevor Homes in 15 found for the Heavyweights boxing Title.

The Year 1982

Albert (Jeepy) Wiggins is back!! I will reflect on the world's most famous landmarks; West Africa, Asia-China, Philippines, Italy, Canada, Norway and The United States.

I was not able to see any locations abroad until I was in the service and out. West Africa also called Western Africa, and the Wes of Africa is the Western most region of Africa. West Africa has been defined as included 18 countries such as Benn-Burkina Faso, the Island Nation of Cape Verde, Gambia, Ghana, Guinea, Bissau, Ivory Coast, Liberia, Mali, Mauritania, Niger, Nigeria, the Island of Sant Helena, Senegal, Sierra Leone, Sao Tome and Principe and Togo. The population of West Africa is estimated at about 362 million people (reported 2016).

The history of East Asia covers the people inhabiting the Eastern subregion of the Asian continent known as East Asia from prehistoric times to the present. The best-known ancient civilization of prehistoric East Asia was China, which flourished in the central plain region and continued until present day.

The history of the Philippines is believed to have begun with the arrival of the first humans using rafts of primitive boats (Balanga Boats) at least 67,000 years ago as the 2007 discovery of Callao man suggested. Negrito tribes first inhabited the Isles, then groups of Austronesians later migrated to the islands.

Italy: The City of Venice is an engineering masterpiece from the well-known St. Mark's Square to the Inf Bridge of Sigh's, the city was entirely on water. The early engineers of the city had a chose specific materials suited to marine conditions and they developed unique techniques for constructing buildings we see today, however, the city of Venice was built in the early 1500 A.D. on a collection of 117 low islands at the center of a lagoon. The numerous canals provided an ideal location for a city because they formed a natural defense against foreign attackers.

Canada: It's history starting with the arrival of Paleo-Indians thousands of years ago to the present-day Canada has been inhabited for Millennia by distinctive groups of Aboriginal peoples with distinct trade networks, spiritual beliefs, and social hierarchies.

Prior to European colonization, the lands starting in the late 15 century, French and British expeditions explored, colonize and fought over various places within North America. In what constitutes present day Canada.

Toronto investors are betting Canada smaller financial firms could see a jump in revenues after the helped fund Marijuana companies ahead of the countries planned legalization of the drug this year.

Equity offerings by Canadian weed companies tripled to a record high of nearly $1 billion in 2017, with nearly two-thirds of that in the final quarter, data from Thomson Reuters Show.

Norway: The Norwegian History. Some important facts in the Norwegian history – most of Scandinavia has covered by ice at least three times, and the last ice melted about 14,000 years ago. The first trace of man in Norway dates to sometime after 10,000 B.C. and they came both from the South and the North.

Facts: Norway introduced Salmon Sushi to the Japanese in the 1980's

United States History:

6 Amendments; 1) Freedom of religion, 2) Right to bear arms, 3) Prohibits the forced quartering of solders during peace time, 4) No unreasonable searches and seizures, 5) No self-incrimination, 6) No double jeopardy.

Note: Historical meaning investigation is the study of the human past. Scholars who write about history are called historians. It is a field of research which uses a narrative to examine and analyze the sequence of events, and it sometimes attempts to investigate objectively the patterns of cause and effect that determine who we are.

The Year 1984:

In 1984 the Aids Virus is identified and is was not the worldwide problem it is today.

Following on from there, the Apple PC releases the Macintosh Computer.

During the widespread famine in Ethiopia many of the top British and Irish, USSR, pop musicians join under the name Band Aid and record the song, "Do They Know It's Christmas".

Following the boycott by the U.S. of the Moscow Olympics, the Soviets block boycott the Los Angeles Olympic Games.

The Recession continue to be a problem in the U.S. and 70 U.S. banks fail in one year.

Also:

1. Yearly inflation rates in USA are 4.3%.
2. Down Jones Industrial Average 1211.
3. The cost of a new house is $86,730.
4. Average income per year is $21,600.
5. Average monthly rent is $350.
6. One gallon of gas is $1.10.
7. Chrysler New Yorker is priced at $13,045.

8. Bacon per pound is $1.69.

9. Movie tickets jumped to $2.50.

10. Apples per pound is .43 cents.

The Year 1985

Politics and History:

Mikhail Gorbachev succeeds Konstantin Chernenko as general secretary of the USSR.

Severe winter in Europe kills more than 100 people.

The United Kingdom starts screening blood donations for the Aids Virus.

The live Aid Rock Concert in London and Philadelphia raises over $600 million for African famine relief.

French sinks the Greenpeace flagship "Rain Warrior" in Auckland, New Zealand.

People who died in 1985:

Orson Wellies, American file-maker.

Rock Hudson, American actor.

Ricky Nelson, American singer and actor.

Yul Brynner, American actor.

The Year 1986 Moving On

1986 was a common year starting on Wednesday of the Gregorian calendar, the 1986 of Common Era and Anno Domini designations; 986th year of the 2nd millennium, the 86th year of the 20th Century and the 7th year of the 1980's decade. The year 1986 was designated as the international year of peace by the United Nations.

Following several trouble-free years in space exploration, the Space Shuttle Challenger explodes shortly after take-off watched by people live on T.V. around the world. The Challenger disintegrates 73 seconds after launching, killing all seven astronauts (including a civilian teacher) on board. (My second wife, Dorothy, was present at this launching, because of her job responsibilities.)

The Internet Mail access protocol defined which open a way for E-Mail.

The human genome project, it launched to understand the human makeup – this will open the way for great advances in the treatment of many illnesses.

The worst ever Nuclear Disaster occurs as the Chernobyl Nuclear Power Station, in Russia, explodes causing the release of radioactive material across much of Europe in the United Kingdom (BSE) commonly known as Mad Cow Disease is identified which causes many deaths over the next few years and a major reform in farming practices.

The Year 1987

During this year: FIJI becomes Republic. The dominion becomes itself as a republic during October. Leading up to the proclamation, FIJI experienced two coups and was run by a military government from May until October. GIJI had become independent from Great Britain in 1870 but Queen Elizabeth II was still the head of state until the establishment of a fully independence for the Republic. FIJI enjoyed full independence for the first time since 1874 when it had become a British colony.

U.S stock market crashes on Monday October 19th with a 508-point drop of 22.6%. Throughout the rest of the world, major drops are recorded by the end of October with Hong Kong dropping by 45.8%.

The USS Stark, a frigate is attached on May 17th and Iraq Air to Sea Missile which is "an accident" and 37 U.S. sailors are killed.

Japan:
Square releases the first "Final Fantasy" video game for the NES in Japan.

US Population:
The U.S. population estimated at 244.6 million.

France:
The Disney Corporation and France agree to create an amusement park World.

The World population reaches approximately five billion (5,000,000,000).

United States:
Soul singer Aretha Franklin was inducted into the Rock and Roll Hall of Fame in January.

Philippines:
Super Typhoon Nina strikes the Philippines submerging 14 fishing villages on the Philippines coast under water leaving 1,000 dead.

Manilla, Philippines Ferry accident resulting in 4,000 dead.

After many years of research, a new drug AZT is used for the treatment of Aides after a long period of growth.

United Kingdom:
In the United Kingdom a major transport disaster happened when a cross-channel ferry capsizes and an underground fire in Kings Cross tube station. England also suffers one of the largest storms in history when hurricane force winds hit much of the South of England.

Other events:

1. 1987, (Roman Numerals MCMLXXXVII) was the 87th year of the 20th century. L987 was not a leap year, and the first day of the year was a Thursday.

2. INF agreement between United States and the USSR eliminates an entire class of nuclear weapons.

3. The drug AZT approved by the U.S. Food and Drug Administration as a treatment for HIV/AIDS.

4. Michael Jackson releases his album "Bad".

5. Kentucky Fried Chicken (KFC) opens its first branch in the People's Republic of China.

6. The first of wreckage from RMS Titanic which sank in 1912.

7. Klaus Barbie goes on trial in Lyon for war crimes committed during the Second World War.

8. Stock market crashes on Black Monday.

9. Portugal sign agreement to return Macau to China in 1999.

The Year 1988

Albert (Jeepy) Wiggins is now 52. Time moves on and my children are growing up – and are now mentally and chronologically: Elizabeth is 31, Stephanie is 28, Gregory is 26, and Valerie is 24.

I was in an agreement with God that I would bring my children up right. And He gave me the momentum and strength to accomplish it.

My employment status has not changed; I am still working as a payroll accountant at MBTA in Massachusetts. My hangout when I would find time was at the Boston Gardens. My life has been a learning experience, and it seems to direct me demographically. And to remove all traces of indolent behavior, my zealous personality motivated me, an gave me a very selected way to behave. I thank God for my health and my sober direction.

The Year 1989

In technology the 486 Series of Microprocessor is released by Intel opening the way for the next generation of much more powerful PC's and Microsoft releases its' Office Suite including spreadsheets, word processor database and presentation software which today still dominates in office applications following.

Massive groups protest the Berlin Wall bringing about the collapse of the Berlin Wall and the East German Government both are dismantled which leads, after many years, to the reunification of East and West Germany.

In China prodemocracy protesters lash with Chinese Security Forces in Tiananmen Square by June 4th and a picture of a man taking on a tank are seen on TV news throughout the world.

Cost of Living in 1989:

1. Yearly inflation rate for the U.S.A. if 4.83%
2. Dow Jones Industrial Average is at 2.753
3. Interest rate for Federal Reserve is 10.50%
4. Cost of a new house is now $120,000.
5. Average income per year is $27,450.
6. Average monthly rent is 4420.
7. Average cost of a new car is 15,350.
8. Cost of gas is .97 cents per gallon.
9. The U.S. postage stamp is .25 cents.
10. Rib Eye Steak is now $3.79 a pound.

Some of the Events in 1989:

- USSR pulls out of Afghanistan.
- PLO and Israel begin preliminary talks.
- Japan Stock Market Crashes.
- South African violence in Black township worsen with over 2,500 killed.
- Serial killer Ted Bundy is executed.
- Egypt – a 4,400-year-old mummy is found in the great Pyramid in Giza.
- The U.SGovernment provides a $150-billion-dollar bail-out for hundreds of savings and loan associations.

The Year 1990

I am now approaching my 54 years of being alive, the thumbprint of distinction was entering my life. As we all know you are responsible for your behavior at age 21, but we all know that life for a conservative thing man has responsibilities to himself, his family and his country. A quadrant of quality and conservative thinking makes you a man. Have I reached the apex or the level of thinking at my age? All I can say is the apex of my thing is now. At my age presently, shattered relationships, disappointments are a way of life that I am familiar with it like an inner compass or a balance of energy. If I could ask for a permanent age to be, I would select 50.

Events happening in 1990:

1. David Dinkins sworn in as the 1st African American Mayor of New York City.

2. FCC implements "SYNDEX" giving independent station more rights over cable TV outlets for exclusive syndicated programs.

3. Jan 2nd Dow Jones hits record 2.800.

4. Jan.3rd, Panama's leader General Manuel Noriega surrenders to U.S. authorities.

5. Jan 7th Tower of Pisa closed to the public due to building leaning too far.

6. Civil Rights activist Reverend Al Sharpton is stabbed in Benson Hurst Brooklyn.

7. 1st elected African American governor is inaugurated. Douglas Wilder of Virginia.

8. 42-year-old George Foreman KOs Gerry Cooney in 2 rounds in Atlantic City, N.J.

9. South Africa says it is reconsidering ban on African National Congress.

10. Jan. 20th – 47th Golden Globes awards go to "Born on the Fourth of July, Tom Cruise film and T.V. awards.

11. South African president F.W. deKlerk promises to free Nelson Mandela and legalizes ANC and 60 other political organizations.

12. Feb 4th – 10 Israeli tourists murdered near Cairo.

13. Larry Bird, Boston Celtics, ends NBA free throw streak of 71 games.

14. Music awards on March 14th Soul Train Music Awards goes to Janet Jackson.

15. Largest art robbery in U.S. history: 13 works of art worth over $500 million are stolen from the Isabella Steward Gardner Museum in Boston, MA. March 18th.

16. March 20th – LA Lakers retired Kareem Abdul-Jabbar's jersey number 33.

17. March 28th, Michael Jordan scores 69 points, 4th time, he scores 60 points in a game.

18. March 28th U.S. president George H.W. Bush awards Jesse Owens the Congressional Gold Medal.

19. April 5th Paul Newman wins a court victory over Julius Gold, to give all profits to charity.

20. April 28th, Boston Celtic score most points in a playoff beating N.Y. Knicks 15-128.

21. March 3rd – Carole Gist (20) is the first African American to be crowned Miss USA in Wichita, Kansas.

22. South Africa, May 2nd) and African National Congress open talks to end apartheid.

23. May 17th – World Health Organization takes homosexuality out of its list of mental illnesses.

24. May 29th – Rickey Henderson steals record 893rd base, breaking Ty Cobb's record.

25. June 5th – South African troops plunder Nelson Mandela's home.

26. Aug. 2nd – U.S. President George H.W. Bush orders troops to Saudi Arabia.

27. Aug. 20th – George Steinbrenner steps don as N.Y. Yankee owner.

28. June 7th – Michael Jackson hospitalized for chest pains.

29. June 23rd – African National Congress leader Nelson Mandela, on a U.S. tour receives a tumultuous welcome in Boston.

30. September 3rd – Jerry Lewis 25th Muscular Dystrophy Telethon raises $44,172,186.

31. Marvin Gaye gets a star on Hollywood's Walk of Fame.

32. October 8th – Israeli police kill 17 Palestinians.

33. Nov. 6th – "I'm Your Baby tonight" third studio album by Whitney Houston is released and made Billboard Album of the Year 1991).

34. Nov. 30th – American actor Burt Lancaster suffers a stroke.

35. Dec. 7th – Ted turner and Jane Fonda announce their engagement.

36. Dec. 9th – the 23rd NAACP Image Awards "Coming To America" wins outstanding motion picture.

CHAPTER 7
(Years 1991-2000)

The Year 1991:

Fragments of the past comes a little clearer as I reach my life stories.

Saddam Hussein dictatorship was exceptionally brutal, with the total number of deaths from purges and genocide conservatively estimated at a quarter of a million people. In 1980, he invaded neighboring Iran which started an ruinous eight years of war that led to no border changes and hundreds of thousands of war dead on both sides. In 1990, he started the Gulf War by invading and annexing Kuwait before being removed by an international coalition led by the United States.

Through the 1990's, Iraq suffered from UN sanctions and isolation. Beginning in the early 2000's, under the Presidency of George W. Bush, Hussein was accused of possessing weapons of mass destruction and was deposed in a 2003 invasion. Though no weapons were found, he was tried for crimes against humanity, and executed in 2006.

The Year 1992:

In technology the first nicotine patch is introduced to help stop smoking and DNA fingerprints is invented.

The continuing Balkan War for the next 3 years between Muslims, Serbs and Croats prompting UN intervention in the UK noting breakouts in cities including Bristol.

In France euro Disney opens.

In the U.S., Bill Clinton becomes President.

The largest Mall in America is constructed spanning 78 acres.

Note: "A humble spirit doesn't look out for its own interest, but instead thinks of other." (This quote describes my wife Dorothy Wiggins' principles.)

The Year 1993:

Albert (Jeepy) Wiggins is now 57 years old.

For the first time, Islamic fundamentalist bomb the World Trade Center.

A devastating tsunami caused by an earthquake off Hokkaido, Japan killing 202 on the small island off Okushim.

The ever-popular Beanie Babies ae launched.

In technology, the first bagless vacuum cleaner is invented.

Intel introduces the Pentium Processor.

More Events:

1. Ferry in Haiti sinks and over 1000 die.
2. Several bombs explode in Bombay India killing about 300.
3. Earthquake centered on Killere Maharashtra India kills nearly 10,000 people.???
4. Nelson Mandela and F.W. deKlerk were awarded the Nobel Peace Prize for their successful efforts to end apartheid.
5. A report states 2.5 million people in Europe are homeless.

6. U.S. anti-abortion activist murders a doctor outside an abortion clinic.

7. The U.S. and Soviet sign agreement to start reducing nuclear warheads by 3,500 each.

8. The average home price is now $67,856. (fact check)??

9. September 11th. Attacks, also referred to as 9/11) were a series of the 4 coordinated terrorists attacks by the Islamic Terrorists group Algida against the U.S. on this morning. The attacks killed 2,996 people, injured over 6,000 others and at least 10 billion in infrastructure and property damage. Two-thirds additional people dies of 9/11 attacks related to cancer and respiratory disease in the months and years following.

Article in the Boston Globe (Newspaper) Sunday Edition:

"President urges resolve, points to Bin Laden. Camp David, Md, as Afghanistan and surrounding states braced for attacks, President Bush asked Americans yesterday to prepare for the sacrifices that prolong conflict may bring. "We're at War", said Bush, who met with his National Security Team at the Presidential retreat here.

"For the first time since Tuesday's serial strikes on, the World Trade Center in New York and the Pentagon, Bush explicitly names Islamic militant Osama Bin Laden as 'a prime suspect.'

"This act will not stand," Bush said, echoing the words of his father, when he wages war in the Persian Gulf a decade earlier.

"We will find those who did it," the President said. "We will smoke them out of their holes. We'll get them running, and we'll bring them to justice."

The year 1994

Albert (Jeepy) Wiggins continues his odyssey. My level of thinking during this period of my life is transforming. I have reached the apex of life. My balance of energy is a metaphor. Timeless principals are shattered, the golden legacy of communication is less, friends and family are gone onto glory.

During this period of my life, is when you correctly advise younger people what is, or will be, the experience you have gained and to share with others by passing through 50 years of living – wide fragments of information to share.

Events of the year:

1. O.J. Simpson is accused of murder.
2. Tonya Harding attacked rival ice skater, Nancy Kerrigan and lost her national figure skating championship title.
3. Start Trek generations is a 1994 Science Fiction Film.
4. Snoop Dogg (Rapper) releases single "Gin and Juice."
5. Palestinian National Authority formed
6. Bill Gates marries Melinda French.
7. Amazon is founded.
8. FDA approves Bayer's Aleve.
9. President Bill Clinton lifts US trade embargo.
10. Medgar Evers' murderer Byron De LaBeckwith sentenced to life in Jackson Mississippi, 30 years after the crime.
11. 21st American Music Awards – Whitney Houston wins.
12. People John Paul II demands juristic discrimination of homosexuals.
13. Arab Terrorist founded guilty of bombing the World Trade Center.
14. Nelson Mandela rejects demand by White Right-Wingers for separate homeland in South Africa.
15. Church of England ordains 1st 33 women priests.
16. Lennox Lewis TKO's Phil Jackson in 8 rounds for the Heavyweight Boxing Title.
17. Rickey Henderson steals his 1,100th career base.

18. Cab Calloway suffered massive stroke at his home in White Plains, N.Y.

19. U.S. reopens Guantanamo Naval Base to process refugees.

20. MLB legend Willie Mays. He won two MVP awards and played in 24 all-Star Games. Growing opinion states that he was possibly the greatest all-around baseball player of all times.

The Year 1995

Events of the year:

Oklahoma City, Oklahoma – exactly two years later after the Waco siege, on April 19th anti-government militant Timothy McVeigh and his co-conspirator Terry Nichols detonated a truck full of explosives outside the Alfred P. Murray Federal Building in Oklahoma City. The blast left 168 people dead and hundreds injured.

1. O.J. Simpson trail. Simpson is acquitted.

2. Israel Prime Minister, Yitzhak Rabin is assassinated.

3. The Million-Man-March occurs in Washington, D.C.

4. eBay is founded.

5. 1995 (roman numerals MCMLXCV.

6. 1995 World Series – Atlanta Braves is the winning team against Cleveland Indians.

7. Microsoft introduces Windows 95.

8. AT&T Inc. is an American Multination conglomerate holding company – the World's largest telecommunications company.

9. This was the first year that the Internet was entirely privatized.

10. More than 170 countries agree to extend the nuclear nonproliferation treaty indefinitely and without conditions.

11. October 3rd, O.J. Simpson is found not guilty of double murder for the deaths of former wife Nicole Simpson and Ronald Goldman.

12. October 16th – the Million-Man-March is held in Washington D.C. – the event was conceived by the Nation of Islam Leader Louis Farrakhan.

As I sit at my computer researching President Mandela's demographics, not everything, certainly smiles and ceremony, there are trials both political and personal for Mandela. And some that combine the personal with political at a cabinet meeting in 1995, He criticizes his Vice President F.W. de Klerk, stating that his predecessor as President and Co-Noble Peace Prize Laureate, is insufficiently supportive of reconciliation. De Klerk at a press conference responds that Mandela's attack on his integrity puts into question all this talk of a National Unity Government.

The Year 1996

Top stories for this year:

1. Israel elects Benjamin Netanyahu.

2. TWO Flight 800 explodes over Long Island, NY, killing 230 people on July 17th.

3. U.S. elects William Clinton.

4. U.S. base bombed in Saudi Arabia, on Tuesday June 25th. A building housing military personnel from the U.S. exploded, killing 19 servicemen and hundreds wounded.

5. Unabomber's favorite targets were universities and airlines, was caught after 18 years. His name is Tec Kaczynski.

6. In the U.K. Prince Charles and Diana Princess of Wales get divorced.

7. Average cost of a new car reaches $16,300.

8. Average house price is $69,453.

9. The U.S. eases sanctions against Cuba.

10. Thirty Black churches in Mississippi are burned to the ground in 18 months.

Albert (Jeepy) Wiggins is now 60. I remember Tupac Shakur was an American rapper and actor, sold over 75 million records world-wide making him one of the best-selling music artists of all times.

Tupac was born to Alice Faye Williams, a member of the Black Panther Party. Tupac's original name is Lesane Parish Crooks. His mother renamed him Tupac Amaru Shakur when he was a year old. He spent most of his childhood on the move with his family. In 1986 they settled in Baltimore, Maryland, where Shakur attended the elite Baltimore School of Arts. He distinguished himself as a student, both creatively and academically, but the family relocated to Marin City, California, before he could graduate. While there, Shakur took to the streets selling drugs and becoming involved in a gang culture that would one day provide material for his rap lyrics.

With increased fame came greater scrutiny of Shakur's gangster lifestyle. A string of arrests culminated with a conviction for sexual assault in 1994, he was incarcerated when his third album, "Me Against the World", was released in 1995. Shakur was paroled after serving eight months in prison and he signed with Suge Knight's Death row Records for his release. That album, "All Eyez On Me" 1996, was a two-disc plan to the "Thug Life", that Shakur embodied. It debuted at number one on the billboard charts and sold more than five million copies within its first year of release. Quick to capitalize on his most recent success, Shakur returned to Hollywood, where he starred in "Bullet" 1996 and "Gridlock" 1997.

On the evening of September 7, Shakur was leaving a Las Vegas casino where he had just attended a prize fight featuring heavyweight champion, Mike Tyson, when he was shot by an unknown assailant. The incident believed by many to be the result of an ongoing rivalry between the East Coast and West Coast rap community, shocked the entertainment world. Shakur dies six days later. More than a decade after Tupac's death remains one of the most recognizable voices in hip-hop history.

The Year 1997:

The number one story of 1997 was a car crash in a tunnel under Paris, three people died. Ordinary, except that victim was Princess Diana, her boyfriend and driver. The fascination and grief unleased by this singular tragedy made it the biggest story of the year according to the Associated Press.

Other deaths figured in the top 10 stories too: the conviction and death sentence of Timothy McVeigh held responsible for 168 obliterated in Oklahoma City.

Mother Teresa. Calcutta wept with the world over Mother Teresa, the revered Roman Catholic nun who ministered to India's poorest of the poor, died of a heart attack at age 87. Her last words were, "Jesus, I love you, I love you," many of her followers walked the muddy streets waiting to pay homage.

Smoked Out. After decades of denying smoking related health problems, tobacco industry leaders were ready to make a deal. Tobacco companies would pay $368 billion if states would drop lawsuits. Amid complex negotiations, congress closed its session without legislation.

Meanwhile, tobacco farmers wanted help. Americans, in polls, doubted that any settlements could reduce teen smoking and documents showed that cigarette makers paid off sympathetic researchers.

1. NASA hauls a picture-perfect Mars landing that produce a series of color and stunning images of the planet.

2. Chinese rule returns to Hong Kong.

3. By Richard Salters: Scientists say that have created the first clone, or genetically identical copy of an adult mammal in the feat that not only would disprove longstanding biological dogma but also raise eerie possibilities of copying human beings.

4. Americans from President Clinton on down sent good wishes to Bobbi and Kenny McCaughey when the Iowa couple's family grew by seven. Gifts ranged from diapers to college tuition.

5. In July, Woolworth's announced it would close its 400 remaining Five & Dime stores nationwide, outflanked by big discounters and abandoned by shoppers preferring suburban malls. For 118 years, the stores sold everything from pet turtles to grilled cheese sandwiches.

6. Tiger Woods wins 1997 Masters with a 9-shot lead to final score of 18. Wins Mercedes championship.

7. How much things cost in 1997;

    a. New house – average cost, $124,100.
    b. Average income is $37,006.
    c. Average monthly rent - $576.
    d. Loaf of bread $1.17.
    e. Movie theatre ticket is $4.59.
    f. One pound of hamburger is $1.38.
    g. Cost of a gallon of gas is $1.22.

The Year 1998

Roman numerals for 1998 – MCMLXCVIII.

This is the year that Black artists changed music as we know it. This year was more than a period where Black hip-hop and R&B musicians released popular projects but was a year that shaped the landscape of the music scene we know today. It was exciting time for hip-hop and R&B. The former got its first Pulitzer Prize, the latter is experiencing a renaissance and the two have joined forces as the mew most popular genre in music. Inevitably, with the hip-hop and R&B largely being held by African American artists, this has ushered in another chapter of Black excellence in music.

The Year 1999.

The 1999 year of the common era (CE) and anno domini (AD) designation – the 999th year of the 2nd millennium, the 99th year of 20th Century and the 10th and last of the 1990's decade. It was designated as the international year of older persons.

1. Gunmen open fire on Shia Muslims worshipping in a mosque in Islamabad, Pakistan, killing 16 and injuring 25.

2. A 6.2 Mw earthquake hits Western Columbia, killing 1900.

3. White supremacist John William King is found guilty of kidnapping and killing African American, James Byrd Jr., by dragging him behind a truck for 2 miles.

4. President Bill Clinton is acquitted in impeachment proceedings in the United States senate February 12th.

5. The brand-new Mandalay Bay Hotel and Casino opens in Las Vegas March 2nd.

6. Bill Gates' personal fortune makes him the wealthiest individual in the world due to the increased value of Microsoft.

7. May 3rd, Oklahoma tornado outbreak a devastating tornado, rated F5 hit Southern and eastern Oklahoma City metropolitan areas, killing 36 people and 5 indirectly. It also produces the highest winds recorded on Earth at 301 miles per hour.

8. July 16th off the coast of Martha's Vineyard, a plane crashes piloted by John f. Kennedy Jr. killing him, his wife Carolyn Bessette Kennedy and her sister Lauren Bessette.

9. Charles Byrd, American jazz musician and classical guitarist dies.

10. Martin Luther King Jr. Day in the United States is established.

The Year 2000

The year 2000 was a century leap year staring on Saturday of Gregorian calendar:

The biggest merges in the country's history, America online agrees to buy Time Warner, the nation's largest traditional media company for $165 billion.

The mega-deal reflects the growing dominance of the internet in areas including publishing, music, film and broadcasting. It also serves to validate the internet proving that the web is likely here to stay and somewhat justifying the value of internet companies that have yet to turn a profit but are worth billions on paper.

1. U.S. Statistics – January 10th
   a. President – William J. Clinton
   b. Vice President albert Gore Jr.
   c. Population 281,421,906

2. Economics:
   a. Federal spending $1,788,83 Billion.
   b. Federal debt $5,674.2 Billion.
   c. Consumer Price Index $172.2 Billion
   d. Unemployment 4.0%
   e. Cost of a first-class stamp $0.34 cents.

3. The State of Vermont passes HB842 legalizing Civil Unions for same sex couples.

4. Egypt – Divers discover the ancient Port of Alexandrea the home of Cleopatra and Mark Anthony.

5. Israel – Pope II visits Israel and prayed forgiveness of the sins of those involved in the Holocaust.

6. Panama – Control of the Panama Canal joining the Pacific and Atlantic Oceans is handed over to Panama after 75 years of U.S. control.

7. A 2,000-year-old tomb reveals mysterious contents. The tomb is believed to be the largest uncovered in Alexandrea, Egypt and has sparked information o speculation about its contents.

8. Torrential rains in Africa lead to the flooding in Mozambique in 50 years which lasted until March and kills 800 people. (Started February 9th until March).

9. Pope John Paul II apologizes for the wrongdoings by members of the catholic church throughout the ages.

CHAPTER 8
(Years 2001-2010)

2001 is the first year of the 3rd millennium, the first year of 21st Century. 2001 was designated as the International Year of Volunteers.

The Boston Globe confronting the side hijacking of American Commercial Airlines by Islamic extremists. Some of the hijackers who became Kamikaze pilots after commandeering two Boston-Los Angeles flights on Tuesday had pilot licenses that suggested that they were sponsored or employed by Saudi Arabian Airlines.

Pakistan agrees to assist if United States can justify targets. What a terrible limbo we are in".

Hollow Horn Bear (1850-1913), was a Brule Lakota leader who fought in many of the battles of the Sioux Wars, including Little Big Horn. As Police Chief of the Rosebud Reservation, he arrested Crow Dog for the murder of Spotted Tail and later testified before the Supreme Court of the United States in Ex parte Crow Dog case. He was the Chief Orator for the Lakota and took part in the inaugural parades for Theodore Roosevelt and Woodrow Wilson. He was featured on a 1922 postage stamp and the 1970 $10 military payment certificate and was possibly his basis for other depictions of Native Americans, including the U.S. five-dollar bill.

Also, in 2001 Al-Qaeda terrorists attack the United States using hijacked passenger aircraft to bring down the Twin Towers in New York and crashing an aircraft into the Pentagon in Arlington County, Virginia leaving nearly 3,000 people dead. The attacks become known simply as 911 due to the date of the attacks September 11th. Due to the attacks several things happen. America declares War on Terrorism and invades Afghanistan where the leader of Al-Qaeda, Osama Bin Laden, was believed to be hiding. Security increase for all aspects of American life including airline security.

1. An earthquake hits Gujarat, India casing more than 20,000 deaths.

2. Timothy James McVeigh is executed for the Oklahoma City bombing.

3. The Leaning Tower of Pisa in Italy reopens to the public during December of 2001. The popular tourist destination was built in 1360 and closed in 1990 for repairs.

4. 2001 becomes known as "Summer of the shark" after several or more attack fatalities.

5. Congo President Laurent Kabila assassinated by bodyguard (Jan 16th. His son Joseph Kabila takes over amid continuing civil war.

6. U.S. spy plane and Chinese jet collide (April 2nd), Sino-American relations deteriorate during a standoff. The 24 crew members of the U.S. plane were detained for 11 days and released after the U.S. issued a formal statement of regret.

7. Race riots in Cincinnati continue for several days following a shooting of an unarmed Black man by White police officer (April 7th).

8. Economics:
   a. Federal spending - $1,864 billion.
   b. Federal debt - $4,807 billion.
   c. Consumer price index - $177.1
   d. Unemployment 4.8%
   e. Cost of a 1st class stamp - $0.34 cents.

9. Women: Venus Williams and Justine Hemin (6-1-3-6-60).

The Year 2002

Nothing has prepared me for the encounter and esoteric behaviors. Culture is individuality and collectivity, and it is an expression of being of vitality, of pride and assertiveness of confidence of pride in a way of life. Observers realize that the public had a sufficient audience, that mistakes of the past are not duplicated. Some things are universal of individuals predicated to being on the wrong side of their thought pattern on purpose. I notice Black people getting to be friends with all races, I notice that different races are starting to blend in with each other located in God's house of prayer, in sports and school. Contradictory is ethnocentrism is becoming gregarious. Maybe not so much political. I am now 66 years old and, in my life, so far, I have met some fantastic people, Black and White.

World Events in 2002:

1. President George Bush's first State of the Union address vows to expand the fight on terrorism and labels Iran, Iraq and North Korea an "Axis of Evil" Jan 29th.

2. March 27th, A Palestinian suicide bomber kills 30 people and injures 140 others at a hotel in Netanya, Israel triggering Operation Defensive Shield, a largescale counter-terrorism operation in the West Bank, two days later.

3. May 25th, A Boeing 747 operation as China Airlines flight 611 breaks up and crashes in the Taiwan Strait, killing all 225 passengers and crew onboard.

4. June 6th, an object with an estimated diameter of 1-0 meters collides with earth over the Mediterranean and deteriorates in mid-air.

5. June 10th, the first direct electronic communication experiment between the nervous system of two humans is carried out by Kevin Warwick in the United Kingdom.

6. July 9th, the organization of African Unity is disbanded and replaced by the African Union.

7. August 26th, Earth Summit 2002 begins in Johannesburg, South Africa, aimed at discussing sustainable development by the United Nation.

8. November 8th, the United Nations Security Council unanimously adopts resolution 1441, forcing Iraq to either disarm or face serious consequences. Iraq agrees to the terms of the resolution on 11/13.

9. March 27th, Milton Berle dies. He was an American comedian.

10. March 27th, Dudley Moore, English pianist, comedian, and actor

The Year 2003

The World population is now 6,326-billion people.

Family is bound together by blood and legal ties, as well as by emotional and social ones. The family is composed by marriage (individuals have rules and regulations), thus marriage is about personal, social and birth rights. The family provides interaction is especially necessary of that will block out the esoteric complication of gossip.

Roxbury Home-Coming & Juneteenth Celebration:

In my hometown of Roxbury, Massachusetts, the Black community leaders came together to form a planning committee for the Roxbury Home-Coming and Juneteenth Celebration. The Committee stated, "We believe the Black community of Boston can and should come together and make this event a holiday that shows pride in our historical backgrounds. We feel that we, as committed community people, can plan and begin to build an event that will eventually prove to be one of the city's most enjoyable historical cultural holidays."

Juneteenth Day is a celebration based on an important event in African American history, the freeing of Texas slaves in 1865, more than two and a half years after the Emancipation proclamation was issued.

The Emancipation Proclamation was officially issued by President Lincoln on January 1, 1863. However, it only freed slaves in states that were rebelling against United States. Once the lawful government was restored, the Union General would announce the proclamation. Texas history has documented and recorded this on June 19, 1865.

Tales attempting to explain the delay of freedom for the Texas slaves have floated back and forth across the country for several years. Whatever the true reasons for the delay, Texas slaves were said to have been freed on June 19, 1865, when General Gordon Granger bolstered by 1800 troops, arrived in the coastal town of Galveston and proclaimed Texas under United States authority.

The Texans had their very first Annual Juneteenth Celebration the next year. Families celebrated by having barbecues, picnics, pageants, parades and baseball games. It was essential African Americans continue to preserve and teach our youth their heritage and the importance of celebrating this event.

If America can celebrate Independence Day, knowing enslaved Black people were not free, she should honor Juneteenth as well. Juneteenth is also known as Juneteenth Independence Day of Freedom.

Roxbury has been celebrating this event now close to 20 years.

P136   ~~P135~~ 161

Roxbury Home-Coming Recognition Dinner
Given by the Shelbune Community Council
April 2002

2

Top News for the Year 2003:

1. World statistics population 4,378-billion people

2. Hiker amputates arm. Mountain climber cuts arm off with pocket-knife after being pinned by boulder for five days. A classic "Water Cooler" story. Could you do the same?

3. Former Iraq President Saddam Hussein is captured by United States forces.

4. China launches Shenzhou 5, their first manned space mission.

5. Michael Jackson is arrested by police on charges of child molestation. He is later acquitted on all charges.

6. SCO Group sues IBM for $1 billion, (later up to $3 billion, then $5 billion) for alleged intellectual property infringements in Linux.

7. U.S. Department of Homeland Security begins operation.

8. 2003 World Series, winning team, Florida Marlins. Losing team was the New York Yankees.

9. The Space Shuttle Columbia is destroyed during re-entry into the atmosphere.

10. A referendum in Sweden results in a vote against forming the Euro Currency Zone.

The Year 2004

I remember the "Gipper." The top story of 2004 was the death of the 40th President of the United States Ronald Reagan at the age of 93 on June 5th at his home in California.

For one week, the World said goodbye to a remarkable leader who dies after a long battle with Alzheimer's. Reagan, "the great communicator," was elected to office in a landslide victory over incumbent Democrat Jimmy Carter in 1980 and is credited with revitalizing the country's stagnant economy and forcing the end of the Cold War during his two terms in office from 1981 to 1989. His charismatic personality and staunch conservatism led the nation in a republican resurgence that kept the GOP in the white House for 12 years.

Reagan remained out of public view since announcing he had Alzheimer's disease in November 1994. He came to symbolize the fight against this disease, which has no cure, during the last decade of his life, Reagan turned the disclosure of his disease into an opportunity to make a final address to the Nation, expressing in an open letter to the American people the same patriotic fervor that had catapulted him into the Presidency. He said, "When the Lord calls me home, whenever that may be, I will leave with the greatest love for this country of ours and eternal optimism for its future," Reagan wrote at the time, "I know that for America, there will always be a bright dawn ahead."

Other events during 2004:

1. Jan 8th, the RMS Queen Mary 2, the largest passenger ship ever built, is christened by her namesake's granddaughter, Queen Elizabeth II.

2. Julia Roberts and Mel Gibson won the People's Choice Awards Motion Picture.

3. Harold Shipman, a British GP who is believed to have killed 200 of his patients in Manchester, is found hanged in his prison cell.

4. January 7th, "Yeah", single release by Usher featuring Lil Jon and Ludacris (Grammy Awards Best Rap/Song collaboration 2005 Billboard Song of The Year 2004)

5. February 1st, two hundred fifty-one people are trampled to death and two hundred forty-four infused in a stampede at the Hajj pilgrimage in Saudi Arabia.

6. February 1st, Wardrobe Malfunction – Janet Jackson's breast is exposed during the half-time sow of super Bowl XXVIII resulting in U.S. broadcasters adopting a stronger adherence to FCC censorship guidelines.

7. February 1st, Super Bowl XXVIII: Tom Brady, Quarterback, led the New England Patriots to beat Carolina Panthers 32-29 at the Reliant Stadium.

8. U.S. Statistics 2004:
    a. President – George Bush.
    b. Vice President Richard Cheney.
    c. Population 294 million.
    d. Nobel Prize for Literature – Elfriede Jelinek.
    e. Song of the Year: Dance with My Father" by Luther Vandross.

The Year 2005

Biography: Pope John Paul II

His life teaching and legacy, Pope John Paul II was the first Polish Pope and the first non-Italian since Adrian VI (1522-1523). The third longest reigning Pope - 26 years. He spoke eight languages and traveled more than any Pope in history, visiting 129 countries. He was a champion of the poor and many credits him with hastening in the fall of communism in Poland and other Eastern Bloc Countries on social issues, such as birth control, women's roles in the church, and homosexuality. He was staunchly traditional which was a source of disappointment among the more liberal elements of the World's 1 billion strong Catholic population. John Paul canonized 482 saints and beatified 1,338 people, believed to be more than all his predecessors combined. He also appointed nearly every member of the College.

of Cardinals who will choose his successor. His birthplace is Wadowice, Poland.

Other Events:

1. Rand Corporation wins award from American Association for Public Opinion Research.

2. Rand Says most public schools managed by Edison Schools match or exceed gains of comparable public schools in 4 to 5 years.

3. Stress from long work hours, rather than deployments, leads to decline in military re-enlistments.

4. Ellen Johnson Sirleaf becomes Africa's first woman elected Head of State 11/11.

5. South Korean cloning scientist Hewing Woo-Suk steps down from Seoul National University after an investigative panel at the University reports he falsified the paper in which he claimed that he cloned 11 human embryos and extracted stem cells from them 12/23.

6. Deaths in 2005:

Anne Bancroft (American Actress), Johnny Carson (Talk Show Host), Shirley Chisholm (American Politician), Richard Pryor (Comedian and Actor), Rosa Parks (American Activist) and Pope John Paul II.

7. 2005 U.S. Statistics:

   a. President – George W. Bush
   b. Vice President – Richard Cheney
   c. Population 296 million

8. January 23rd, Johnny Carson – American television host's death date.

9. February 14th, former Lebanese prime Minister Rafik Harim is assassinated along with 21 others by a suicide bomber in Beirut.

10. December 26th, a 9.0 magnet earthquake, the largest earthquake in 40 years ruptured the floor of the Indian Ocean off the Coast o the Indonesian Island of Sumatra. The earthquake triggered the Tsunami so powerful that the waves caused casualties on the Coast of Africa and were detected as far as the East Coast of United states. The death remains uncertain, but most estimates state that the final tally will exceed 225,000, making it by far, the deadliest tsunami in history. Eleven countries bordering the Indian Ocean – all relatively poor and vulnerable -suffered devastation and millions were left homeless. Hardest hit were Indonesia, Sri Lanka, India, and Thailand. It is the largest earthquake ever recorded.

The Year 2006

Events of this year: Coloplast CEO Sten Scheibel joined Governor Paurlenty and Minneapolis Mayor R.T. Ribak to its new corporate campus on West River Road in North Minneapolis. The move beginning with the first 200 jobs in September will enable them to double the size of its company and facilitate up to 500,000 square feet for office research and development and production activities.

Coloplast is a world leader in the design and manufacturing of high and innovative health care products and services," Governor Pawlenty said. "Their decision to come to Minnesota is an important and exiting development that underscores yet again are commitment to placing Minnesota squarely at the intersection where medial technology and biosciences converge to create a bio-business revolution.

The company specialized in urology and continence care, ostomy care, chronic wound care, skin care and breast care products and services. It employs nearly 7,000 people worldwide, including about 90 people at Coloplast skin care products in North Mankato. Coloplast's recent acquisition of mentor's Urology Division added ab out 330 employees in Minneapolis, which will provide foundation for its U.S. Operations.

"With our higher quality of life and growing life sciences industry, Minneapolis is a perfect home for Coloplast," Mayor Rybak said. "As the commercial hub of the upper Midwest, Minneapolis will do everything it can to ensure that Coloplast has the workforce and financial support it needs to succeed in North Minneapolis."

"Once we complete the acquisition of Mentor, the decision to move our North American headquarters to Minneapolis was an easy one." Scheibel said, "Its clear that Minnesota's leaders continue to be visionary and aggressive in building upon an already strong global presence in medical technology and the biosciences we're delighted to be here and make Minnesota our home."

Other Events in 2006:

1. The World Wide Web became a tool for bringing together the small contributions of millions of people and making them matter more.

2. World Statistics: Population 4,378 billion.

3. The Asian tsunami focused its worst destruction on the Northern Indonesian province of Aceh, killing more than 130,000 people and leaving half a million homeless.

4. Morgan Stanley annual Healthcare Conference was held in New York City.

5. January 25th the Walt Disney Company buys Pixar Animation Studios from Lucas Film LTD for 7.4 billion and now Pixar is a subsidiary of Walt Disney Pictures.

6. January 19th - NASA launches the first space mission to Pluto as a rocket hurls the new Horizons Spacecraft on a nine-year journey.

7. January 17th, a massive mudslide occurs in Southern Leyte, Philippines, killing an estimated 1,126 people.

8. March 10th, NASAs Mars Reconnaissance orbit around Mars.

9. October 9th, North Korea claims to have conducted its first ever nuclear test.

10. November 5th, former President of Iraq Saddam Hussein is sentenced to death by hanging by Iraqi special tribunal.

The Year 2007

Speaker of the House Nomination: In the 2006 midterm elections, the Democrats took control of the House, picking up31 seats on November 16, 2006. Nancy Pelosi was unanimously chosen by her caucus as the Democratic candidate for speaker, effectively making her speaker elect. While the Speaker is elected by the full House membership, in modern practice the election is a formality since the Speaker always comes from the Majority party.

This is a historic moment for the Congress and for the women of this country. It is a moment for which we have waited more than 200 years, never losing faith. We waited through the many years of struggle to achieve our rights. But women were not just waiting, women were working. Never losing faith, we worked to redeem the promise of America, that all men and women are created equal. For our daughters and granddaughters today, we have broken the marble ceiling. For daughters and our granddaughters, the ski is the limit, anything is possible for them.

Other events:

1. The 79th Academy Awards nominations: Dreamgirls, Babel, Pan's Labyrinth, The Queen, and The Departed.

2. Gordon Brown replaces Tony Blair as Minister of Great Britain June 27th.

3. The African National Congress choses Jacob Suma as its leader, ousting South African President Thabo Mbeki December 18th.

4. Romania and Bulgaria join the European Union, bringing the number of member nations to 27, January 1st.

   a. A. Federal Spending = $14.074 Billion.

   b. B. Federal Debt = $9229 Billion.

   c. C. Consumer Price Index 2102.

   d. D. Unemployment 4.6%.

5. Record of year: "Not Ready to Make" Dixie Chicks.

6. Miss America: Lauren Nelson of Lawton Oklahoma.

7. Cristina Fernandez de Kirchner is elected Argentina's first woman President.

8. President Ramous-Horta names independent activist Xanana Gusmao as Prime Minister of East Timor August 5th.

9. Romani join the European Union bringing the number of number nations to 27, January 1st.

The Year 2008

Selected Massachusetts Case law:

Adoption of a minor 373 (2015) "Law parentage and its associated rights and responsibilities is conferred by statute on the consenting spouse of a married couple whose child is conceived by one woman of the marriage, through the use of assisted reproductive technology consented to by both women." See G.L.C. 46 Sec. 4B.

Delia Corte Vs Ramirez 81 Mass. App. Ct. 906 (2012):

A child born of a same sex marriage is the legitimate child of both people. "As a result, it follows that when there is a marriage between same sex couples, the need for that second parent adoption to, at the very least, confer legal parentage on the non-biological parent is eliminated when the child is born of the marriage."

Ella-Warnken Vs Ella 463 Mass 29 (2012):
"A Vermont civil union is the functional equivalent of a marriage." "Therefore, a Vermont civil union must be dissolved prior to either party entering into marriage with a third person in the commonwealth."

The Presidency of Barack Obama:
The Presidency of Barack Obama began at noon est. on January 20, 2009, when he was inaugurated as the 44th President of the United States and ended on January 20th, 2017. Mr. Obama, a Democrat, took office following a decisive victory over Republican John McCain in the 2008 Presidential election. For years later, in the 2012 election, he defeated Republican Mitt Romney to win re-election. He was the first African American President, the first multiracial President, the first non-white President, and the first President to be born in Hawaii. Barack Obama was succeeded by Republican Donald Trump, who won the 2016 Presidential election.

President Obama's first term actions addressed the global financial crisis and included a major stimulus package, a partial extension of the Bush tax cuts, legislation to reform health care. A view on some high-profile social issues shifted rapidly: eight states and District of Columbia legalized marijuana for recreational purposes, a legal shift accompanied by a striking reversal in public opinion. For the first time on record, most Americans now support legalization of the drug.

Obama's election quickly elevated America's image abroad, especially in Europe where George W. Bush was deeply unpopular following the U.S invasion of Iraq. In 2009, shortly after Obama took office, residents in many countries expressed a sharp increase in confidence in the ability of the U.S President to do the right think in international affairs. While Obama remained largely popular internationally throughout his tenure, there were exceptions, included in Russia and key Muslim nations. And Americans themselves became more wary of international engagement.

The U.S economy is much better shape now than it was in the aftermath of the great recession, which cost millions of Americans their homes and jobs and led Obama to push through a roughly $800 Billion stimulus package as one of his first orders of business. Unemployment has plummeted from 10% in late 2009 to below 5% today; The Dow Jones Industrial Average has more than doubled.

More Events for 2008:

1. The U.S. Supreme Court rules 5 to 4 that prisoners at Guantanamo Bay Cuba, have a right to challenge the detention, in Federal Court.

2. November 4th, Democratic Senator Barack Obama wins the Presidential election.

3. November 4th, Voters in California narrowly pass a ballot measure proposition 8 that overturns the May 15th, 2008 California Supreme Court decision that same sex couples have the constitutional right to marry.

   a. Median Household income; $50,303 Billion.

   b. Consumer Price Index: 215.3 billion.

   c. Unemployment 5.8%

4. Superbowl: N.Y. Giants defeated New England Patriots.

5. World Series: Phil. Phillies defeat Tampa Bay.

6. NBA Championship Boston Celtics defeated L.A. Lakers.

7. Books: "Audacity of Hope", Barack Obama.

The Year 2009

January 15th, U.S. Airways plane river landing:

1. Rescue boats float near a U.S. Airways plane floating in the water after crashing into the Hudson Ricer in the afternoon on this date in

New York City. The Airbus 320 flight 1549 crashed shortly after take-off from LaGuardia Airport heading to Charlotte, North Carolina.

2. The path to justice has a beginning. We are here to move forward with you.

3. The first step in safeguarding tomorrow but often the distinction between legal and illegal, right and wrong, get lost in a web of complicated rhetoric.

4. Types of fraud:

    Medicare and Medicaid Fraud

    Pharmaceutical Fraud

    Education and Grant Fraud

    Banking and Financial Services Fraud

    Securities and Exchange Commission Fraud

    Defense Contractor Fraud

    Tax Fraud

5. Does the anti-retaliation protection extend to me if I am not an employee of the company at issue? It may.

6. Johnson and Johnson agree to then largest false Claims Act Settlement in Risperdal lawsuits: In 2013 the U.S. Justice department announced that Johnson and Johnson would pay $1.273 Billion to the Federal Government.

7. June 25th Michael Jackson dies after being taken to a hospital having suffered cardiac arrest according to the Los Angeles County Coroner's office.

8. January 20th, Barack Obama launches his Presidency before an estimated 1.5 million people.

9. Police reported – as many as 20 were present at gang rape outside a school dance.

10. June 4th, American actor, David Carradine is found dead, hanging by a nylon rope in a hotel room closet in Bangkok, Thailand.

An Inauguration to Remember:

On January 20th Barack Obama became the 44th U.S. President. He also became the first African American to lead the country. When Obama took his oath of office, a crowd of 2 million people came to watch the ceremony. That made it the biggest event ever held in Washington D.C. The crowd stood for hours in freezing cold temperatures to share in this special day.

September 15th: President Barack Obama wrote a letter to Joseph Lowery, Civil Rights Activists and Pastor, for his birthday.

The President said in his letter, "Michelle and I send our best wishes to you on your 88th birthday. We hope you enjoy celebrating this special occasion with family and friends."

"Throughout our Nation's history, visionary men and women have stood up to fulfill America's promise of equality for all. Alongside De. Martin Luther King and Reverend Abernathy, you laid the groundwork for the Civil Rights Movement, carrying forth a legacy that touched America's conscience and changed its history."

"When you delivered the benediction at my Inauguration, your powerful call for a new beginning of unit echoed in the heart of all who joined us on that day. In recognition of your lifetime of service, it was my great privilege to present you with the presidential Medal of Freedom, our Nation's highest civilian honor. Only by standing on the shoulders of giants like you could I reach the office I hold, and countless Americans join me in honoring your remarkable contributions to our country."

"Again, happy birthday. I hope you are blessed with many more joyful years."

I was there on this very day of Reverend Joseph Lowrey's birthday celebration. Present were many celebrities, like Aretha Franklin and Samuel Jackson, political representatives, community activists and students from Clark Atlanta University, Morehouse and Spellman Colleges.

A New Justice:

In May, President Obama chose Judge Sonia Sotomayor to sit on the U.S. Supreme Court. The Supreme is the most powerful court in the land. The U.S. Senate confirmed Obama's choice. In September, Sotomayor was sworn into office. She is the first Hispanic and the third woman to sit on high court. There are nine Supreme Court Justices. Together, their decisions carry the weight of law.

The Year 2010

1. Greatest mortgage reduction program in the U.S. history is set to expire in 2018, but the banks have been keeping this a secret? Check out the Harp approval Website.

2. President Obama announcing the Harp Refinance to help Americans save money.

3. Doris Day is almost 100 years old and she keeps herself super fit.

4. U.S. Statistics for 2010:

    a. President – Barack Obama

    b. Vice President – Joe Biden

    c. Population 310 million

    d. Life expectancy 78.2

5. November 23rd, the military of North Korea unexpectedly attacks the Island of Yeonpyeong in south Korea, killing two civil and two marines. Eighteen others are wounded. This is the first North Korea has fired on a civilian target since the suspension of the Korean War in 1953.

6. May 5th, a Picasso painting sells for a record-creaking $106.5 Million at a Christie's auction. The painting, "Nude Green Leaves and Bust", depicts Picasso's mistress was painted in 4 days.

7. November 22nd, at least 300 people were killed and hundreds more injured in a stampede during Cambodia's annual Water Festival. The stampede reportedly occurred after people panicked when a densely crowded bridge began to sway.

8. Goldman Sachs has agreed to $550 Million settlement with the Federal Government after being accused of misleading investors during the Supreme Mortgage crisis and housing market collapse.

9. Super Bowl: The New Orleans Saints defeated the Indianapolis Colts 32-17.

10. Wimbledon - Serena Williams defeated Vera Zvonareva 6-3, 62.

The Good, the Bad and the Ugly of turning 50 for women:

Before turning fifty, its possible for a woman to look forward and believe he majority of her years still lie ahead after all, the average life expectancy for a woman in the U.S. now exceeds 80 years. But after turning fifty, nearly all of us are closer to death than birth. (Linda Lowen). That thought can be both sobering and liberating. Sobering because it reminds us there is a finite span in which to accomplish what we want, be it a lengthy bucket list or a few simple wants and desires. Liberating because when we mentally and emotionally grasp that truth, a lot of non-essential concerns drop away, and the important things come to the forefront.

The downside of turning 50:

Turning 50 heralds a decade of transitions, many of them involving bodily changes. Menopause ends the childbearing years. Gray hairs supplant natural color, forcing one of three decisions: let nature take its course, cover the gray, or try to a completely different shade. Changes in vision require reading glasses. Gravity takes its toll. Our necks sag, stomachs bulge, breasts drop, faces wrinkle, underarms swing, waist thicken and knees and back ache. The skin loves its elasticity, causing some of you to try and turn the clocks back by means of all sorts of chemical and medical interventions, such as moisturizers, wrinkle creams, Botox injections, plastic surgery, face and eye lifts. Exterior factors also push you in a direction. The empty net that results when children leave for college or work leave, may initially seem depressing. But in the long run, the freedom can be exhilarating, providing an opportunity to try something new such as a career change, going back to school, or downsizing and moving to a new location.

Seeing 50 as a New Beginning:

Turning 50 is certainly momentous, but it does not have to be pretentious. It can be a time in which to evaluate what is important and what not and decide it, where and when change I needed.

Fifty is not the end of the world, but a threshold that opens onto new horizons. Whether you view the landscape ahead of you with optimism and hope or regret and fear may determine whether you reach those milestones of 60, 70, 80, 90 or beyond. Perhaps the best news of all is this: with women outliving men in most nations around the globe, the benefits of your gender finally outweigh the drawbacks. (Linda Lowen).

CHAPTER 8

(Years 2011-2020 – the remaining decade)

Year 2011

Events of this year:

1. Nearly a decade after the 9/11 terrorist attacks, Osama Bin Laden is killed.

2. The death of Moammar Gadhafi was a brutal tyrant leading a country where the slightest dissent of free expression was not tolerated.

3. December 11th, North Korean dictator, Kim Jong II dies of a heart attack.

4. The United Nations estimated that at least 12 million people have been affected by the drought and famine across Somalia, Kenya, Ethiopia and Djibouti.

5. In a year of death and drama, there was a bit of good news that sent viewers around the world flocking to their TV sets. On April 29th, Prince William and Kate Middleton said their vows in Westminster.

6. July 10th, with a eulogy proclaiming what British tabloids newspaper brought down one of the oldest jewels in Rupert Murdock's moisturizers, ointments to reduce age spots, wrinkle creams, Botox injections, plastic surgery, face and eye lifts.

7.   Greece is on the brink of a meltdown due to spiraling debt, and the deficit crisis. Last year (2010, the international fund bailed out Greece.

8.   Norway shootings a rightwing extremist detonated a powerful bomb outside the Prime Minister's headquarters in Oslo, Norway, on July 22nd, killing 8 people and then two hours later killed 69.

9.   Top 10 New Hip-Hop artists of 2011: Big Sean, Preemo, L.E.P., Bogus Boys, the Nice Guys, Boog Brown, Kendrick Lamar, Cyhi da Pryce, Big K.R.I.T, Ofwgkta and Danny Brown.

10. May 2nd, Osama Bin Laden's death at the hands of U.S. Forces were announced by President Barack Obama. Bin Laden is believed to have ordered the attacks on New York and Washington on September 11, 2001. It was the third busiest day on the BBC News website in 2011, with 11.7 million browsers. "Al-Qaeda Leader Osama Bin Laden has been killed by U.S. forces in Pakistan," President Barack Obama has said. Bin Laden was shot dead at a compound near Islamabad, in a ground operation based on U.S. intelligence, but thee first lead for which emerged last august. Mr. Obama said, "U.S. Forces took possession of the body after a firefight." Bin Laden was top on the U.S. "Most Wanted" list. "DNA test later confirmed that Bin Laden was dead", U.S. officials said.

Bin laden was buried at sea, after a Muslim funeral on board an aircraft carrier, Pentagon officials said. Announcing the success of the operation, Mr. Obama said it was "The most significant achievement to date in our nation's effort to defeat Al-Qaeda". The U.S. has put its embassies around the world on alert warning Americans of the possibility of Al-Qaeda reprisal attacks for Bin Laden's killing.

CIA director, Leon Panetta, said Al-Qaeda would "almost certainly" try to avenge the death of Bin Laden.

Crowd gather outside the White House in Washington D.C. chanting, "USA, USA after the news broke.

U.S. secretary of State, Hillary Clinton said, "The operation sent a signal to the Taliban in both Afghanistan and Pakistan.

"You cannot wait us out, you cannot defeat us, but you can make the choice to abandon Al-Qaeda and participate in a peaceful political process." She said.

Clinton also said, "There was no better rebuke to Al-Qaeda and its heinous ideology across the Arab world against authoritarian governments."

Bin Laden, 54, approved the 9/11 attacks in which nearly 3000 people dies. He evaded the forces of the U.S. and its allies for almost a decade, despite a $25 Million bounty on his head.

President Obama took action!

The Year 2012

This was a year to truly remember. In 1957, the child that I fathered in the Philippines, found me on Facebook!! I am not too much of a fan for social media and rarely look at my page. My youngest daughter called to ask if I had another child, in addition to the three, because on the Boston Group Postings, a young woman was asking about me and if anyone could give her some leads. Through the private messaging section, I was able to ask specific questions and determined that she was the one I had longed to reconnect for many years. Elizabeth who now lives in Maryland, made plans to visit this same year. What a blessing!

Events of the Year.

1. Gun attack at Crimea Collage kills 19: An 18-year-old student was behind the shooting, investigators in the Russian annexed Region said.
2. Bing-YouTube:
3. Get the answers you need with everyday intelligence from Bing and transform you cooking mishaps into a culinary triumph.

4. Pentagon admits it had a UFO Program, claims it ended 2012: The news and stories that matter, delivered weekday mornings. Subscribe Washington – the Pentagon said on Saturday that its long secret UFO investigation program ended in 2012, when U.S. Defense Officials shifted attention and funding on other priorities.

5. United Kingdom: The diamond Jubilee of Queen Elizabeth II celebrating the 60th anniversary of her ascension to the throne in 1952 takes place, with celebrations throughout the year in the United Kingdom and around the world.

6. A gunman opens fire at a midnight screening of "The Dark Knight Rises" movie in Aurora, Colorado, killing twelve and injuring fifty-eight people on July 20th. Th suspected shooter, James Holmes, was captured by police and his trial was scheduled for February of 2014.

7. The Mars Science Laboratory or "Curiosity Rover" successfully lands on Mars.

8. Austrian, Felix Baumgartner, becomes the first person to break the sound barrier without mechanical assistance when he jumps over New Mexico on October 14th.

9. The film "Marvels the Avengers" is released and becomes one of the highest grossing films.

10. Hurricane Sandy devastates the U.S. East coast and Caribbean killing around two hundred people in October.

11. Cost of living in 2012:

    a. Cost of a new house $263,200.
    b. Average monthly rent $1,045.
    c. Cost of a gallon of gas #3.91.
    d. Movie tickets $8.20.
    e. One dozen of eggs $1.54.
    f. Load of brad $1.88.

The year 2012 is the year of the Dragon and it will arrive in February Chinese Astrology year is on February 4th.

Vladimir Putin: Russian President while his rule of has seen the economy, general living standards and levels of law and order improve.

Drastically since he took office after the economy, collapse of the 1990s, he has been criticized domestically and abroad for his increasingly authoritarian rule, his intervention in Ukraine and for perceived level of corruption in the Russian government.

Historical Events in the life of Vladimir Putin:

October 1, 1998 - Vladimir Putin became a permanent member of the security council of the Russian Federation.

August 5, 2008 – Dmitay Medvedev appoints Putin as Russian Prime Minister.

April 3, 2012 – Putin wins Russian Presidential election amid allegations of voter fraud.

December 28, 2012 Vladimir Putin signs into law a ban on U.S. adoption of Russian children.

While Putin's rule in Russia has seen the economy, general living standards and levels of law and order improve drastically since he took office after the economy collapse of the 1990's, he has been criticized domestically and abroad for his increasing authoritarian rule.

The Year 2013

Boston Marathon bombing of this year, Terrorist attack that took place a short distance from the finish line of the Marathon on April 15th. A pair of homemade bombs detonated in the crowd watching the race, killing 3 people and injuring more than 260.

The pressure cooker bombs detonated 12 seconds and 210 yards apart at 2:49 pm, near the finish line of the race, killing three people and injuring several hundred others, including 16 who lost limbs. Three days later, the Federal Bureau of Investigation released images of two suspects, who were later identified as Kyrgyz – American brothers Dzhokhar Tsarnaev and Tamerian Tsarnaev. They killed an MIT policeman. Tamerian died after a gun battle with police.

The trial held in July Dzhokhar pleaded not guilty to the 30 Federal charges against him, including the use of a weapon of mass destruction resulting in death.

Other events:

1. Thinking the unthinkable in China abandoning North Korea.

2. Target settles 2013 hacked customer data breach for $18.5 Million.

3. The President signs the American Taxpayer Relief Act of 2012 averting a "fiscal cliff" that threatened to plunge the nation back into recession. The law also extends expiring jobless benefits and blocks cuts in Medicare.

4. "A 5 to 7 percent weight loss lessens the risk of developing diabetes if one has prediabetes."

5. What doctors do not know about menopause: Three out of four women who seek help for symptoms do not receive it. (according to Jennifer Wolff, AARP)

6. The new words "Twerk" and "selfie" were added to the dictionary.

7. March 13th Pope Francis became the first Pope to emerge from Latin America.

8. April 17th, an explosion at the fertilizer plant in West Texas, killed 15 people, nine who were first responders.

9. The trial that divided the country was of George Zimmerman, a Florida man who killed Trayvon Martin, a teenager.

10. Description of Nelson Mandela's Legacy

    a. Freedom Fighter Leader

    b. God-like humanitarian human rebel

    c. Civil Rights Icon

    d. Giant among men.

    e. Hero, Peacemaker, Wise and Brave.

    f. Statesman Courageous Revolutionary

    g. Inspiration, Visionary activist, Liberator.

The Year 2014

The deadliest outbreak during this time was Ebola, a deadly hemorrhagic fever, started in West Africa in the Spring of 2014 and began to spread rapidly in late summer. Most of the epidemic was contained in three countries -

Guinea, Sierra Leone and Liberia – though there have been cases confirmed in at least five other countries, including two diagnosed in the United States.

The latest World Health Organization figures report that 6,000 people have died from the outbreak out of more than 17,000 total cases. The contagious disease created a global epidemic that has not yet been contained.

The United Nations Security Council declared the Ebola virus outbreak in West Africa "A threat to international peace and security" and unanimously adopted a resolution urging U.N. member states to provide more resources to fight the outbreak.

Black Lives Matter:

Eric Garner, John Crawford, Michael Brown, Ezell Ford, and Tamir Rice. These are just a few of the names of black people killed by police on American streets, most of them unarmed, some of them teenagers a young as 12 years old, some of them left faced down in the middle of the street for hours, and they are on the minds of many Americans who have stood up across the country in sadness and outrage over a long history of brutal tactics by police that have wrongly claimed the lives of many before them.

Their deaths have sparked nationwide protests by people of all political and social stripes who are demanding police reform and telling the world that Black Lives Matter. With the power of twitter, Instagram and other platforms, people across the United States are still organizing and marching for change.

In the wake of Michael Brown's shooting to the hands of a Missouri police officer, Americans also witnessed another dark side of the growing police state. The rapid militarization of local police across the country. We should all be deeply disturbed by the fact that an unarmed African American man is an astoundingly seven times more likely to be killed by American police than an unarmed White man.

If you think that Black Lives Matter, then you should be working for school reform, economic growth, and, yes, more effective law enforcement and crime prevention measures to protect Black communities, which suffer an enormous disproportionate share of crime and violence. Never mind the stagecraft; that is what you do if you think Black Lives Matter.

Other Events for 2014

1. Americans believe the internet has made them better informed.

2. Ebola epidemic becomes global health crisis.

3. The prospect of a Malaysian Airlines 747 plane filled with 239 missing people on bord have never been found and the search continued to this day.

4. Heightened tension following the kidnapping and murder of three Israeli teens led to an exchange of rocket fire, resulting in a formal Israeli offensive against Hamas in the Gaza Strip. The rocket fire lasted seven weeks.

5. Protest erupted nationwide after a grand jury decided in late November not to indict White police officer, Darren Wilson, in the shooting death of Michael Brown in Ferguson, Missouri.

6. Erick Garner's death was captured on video and his last words - "I can't breathe" have become a rallying call for protesters.

7. Three leaders of ISIS were killed by American airstrikes in Iraq in the past six weeks, U.S. defense officials say.

8. U.S. Cuba thaw: The Obama Administration was normalizing Cuba's Cold War Era ties. The decision came after 18 months of secret talks

hosted by Canada, and which included the influential support of Pope Francis.

9. Robin Williams' suicide: One of the most beloved American comedian-actor of the last few years, took his own life at his home in Tiburon, California at the age of 63.

10. Rapper and record producer Kanye West, 36, weds model Kim Kardashian,33, at Fort Di Belvedere in Florence, Italy.

Twelve reasons Why Obama is One of the Best Presidents Ever: Matthew Lynch, Ed.D.

Mr. Lynch stated in his blog, *"I have yet to find the words to describe the overwhelming sense of satisfaction I felt on November 4, 2008 when Obama won the popular vote by 53 percent. With tears in my eyes, and joy in my heart, I stood alongside people of color across the nation as we celebrated Americas first inauguration of a black president. As a young black man, I felt a true sense of patriotism as I witness our country rally together to show, finally, that we are more concerned about who I the most qualified man for the job, regardless of race or age. As Obama so simple, yet eloquently, stated during his celebration speech - change had come to America – a change we so desperately needed after eight painful years of George W. bush's colossal failure as our nation's leader.*

He continues, "A lot has happened since then. I am loyal to the Democratic Party and to my president, but I am not blind, deaf or dumb. I recognize that Obama has made more than one controversial decision and rocked the boat a time or two during his presidency. Sure, he has committed his share of blunders and tripped over his own words from time to time. But there is not a president in American history who did not flub up big time at some point during his administration. While I acknowledge he has made several mistakes in recent years, I stand firm in my conviction that Barack Obama is one of the greatest presidents America has ever seen. I believe history will prove this, and with time, he will be remembered in the annals of history as a revered revolutionary."

Here are 12 reasons why Obama is one of the best presidents ever:

1. *He is for the People. Unlike many presidents who preceded him, he cares about what is best for the greater good. His actions have always been motivated by a sincere desire to do what is best for the majority, even if it meant losing ground with the wealthy, influential or powerful minority.*

2. *He is for civil rights. He has consistently spoken on behalf of the disenfranchised, the underdog and the most controversial members of society – even though it was politically unpopular to do so at the time. His outspoken support of gay marriage is an excellent example. Gay marriage is and has always been a legal and civil rights issue – not a moral one as conservatives would have you believe.*

3. *He is for one race; the human race. In just a few short years. Obama's professional achievements and continued demonstration of equality and integrity have done wonders for race relations. America has never been more unified as a people than it has been under the direct leadership of Barack Obama. Finally, the racial lines that have divided blacks and whites for decades seem to be narrowing.*

4. *He is for a healthcare system that brings hope and healing to the hurting. Obama's healthcare plan has allowed uninsured Americans to reap the benefits of a universal healthcare system.*

5. *He is for the middle class. Here are just a few of the comments made by President Barack Obama in recent months: "Rebuilding our economy starts with strengthening the middle class. Extending tax breaks on 98 percent of families now would give hardworking Americans the security and confidence they need." In July 2012, during a visit to Cedar Rapids, Iowa, he said, "The vision of a strong middle class is what we're fighting for. What we need is somebody who is going to fight every single day to grow the middle class because that is how our economy grows, from the middle out, from the bottom up, where everybody has got a shot. That's how the economy grows."*

6. *He is for women's rights. Obama's very first executive action as President was to sign the Lilly Ledbetter Fair Pay Act, a bill specifically designed to annihilate wage discrimination barriers for women. He*

also fully funded the Violence Against Women Act, which addressed the criminality of sexual assault and domestic violence an provides women with the services needed to overcome such atrocities. President Obama nominated two women to the supreme Court, including the first Latina justice in American history. Furthermore, Obama has taken exceptional measures to secure grant money for women business owners and get them a fair shake from the Small Business Administration.

7. *He is for doing away with pomp and circumstance. As the 44th president of the United States, he has changed the face of the Oval Office forever. Many suggest Obama's casual demeanor and informal interaction with the American people is inappropriate, and even downright offensive. Millions of people perceive his relaxed deportment, humorous candor and outright honesty as a breath of fresh air. Although he is a politician, and the president there is something about him that makes him real and relatable. Even though he is the most powerful man in the world, he is, at heart, just a man.*

8. *He is for the environment. President Barack Obama has taken a forward-thinking approach to creating a red, white, blue and green America. His policies and initiatives for a clean energy economy have had an incredible impact on the future of the nation. For instance, the U.S. reduced oil imports by more than 10 percent from 2010-2011. That's more than 1 million barrels a day. The Administration continues to seek ways to reduce America's dependence on oil, promote efficient energy and invest in clean energy practices.*

9. *He is for veterans. Obama has consistently promoted the allocation of funds, increased benefits, job opportunities and extended resources for our nation's veterans. Although Obama never served in the U.S. Armed forces, he has always been a responsible and thoughtful commander-in-chief. He has never lost sight of the commitment, dedication and sacrifice made by the brave men and women who volunteer for military service and he has been adamant about rewarding them accordingly.*

10. *He is for peace. Let us never forget that Barack Obama was awarded the Nobel Peace Prize in 2009, one of the greatest accomplishments any man or woman could hope to achieve in a lifetime. The award reads, "The Nobel Peace prize for 2009 is to be awarded to President Barack Obama for his extraordinary efforts to strengthen international diplomacy and cooperation between peoples. The Committee has attached special importance to Obama's vision of and work for a world without nuclear weapons." During his presidency, Obama successfully ended the war in Iraq and is close to finally putting an end to the conflict in Afghanistan and bring our troops home for good.*

11. *He is for education. Obama has always been an advocate for education, making it a top priority during his administration. Believing education is what brings about the strength of a nation. Obama has set a goal for the U.S. to have the highest proportion of college graduates in the world by 2020. He has increased federal funding and doubled the amount of grant money allocated to students seeking a higher education to cover rising tuition costs. During his presidency, Obama also passed the White House Initiative on Educational Excellence for African Americans and the White House Initiative on educational Excellence for Hispanics to ensure equal education for people of color.*

12. *He is for entertaining the masses. If we must listen to a president yakity-yak about this or that for another four years, we might as well pick one with charisma and charm. If you can't find anything else appealing about Obama, you can't deny the fact that the guy is an amazing speaker with wit, fantastic comedic timing and an incredible intellect. In fact, I will go so far as to say when the man does finally retire from politics, he has a rewarding and lucrative job as a stand-up comic waiting him if he so chooses. When is the last time you heard a president joke about drinking beer, belt out All Green with poise and precision at a moment's notice and admit to watching the Kardashians?*

Lynch stated, "If there 12 reasons aren't enough to convince that President Obama is one of the best presidents ever, then you are not thinking objectively!"

Matthew Lynch Ed.D – author of "The Call to Teach" and editor of the Edvocate.

The Year 2015

President Barack Obama:

Businesses added 13.7 million new jobs over a 69-month streak of job growth. Mr. Obama also cited the latest unemployment rate figures in October, it fell to 5 percent and has remained at that level since, as proof of a strong economy.

Despite numerous Republican threats and challenges to the Affordable care Act (ACA), the president's landmark health bill survived 2015. In June, the supreme Court even upheld a major part of the Obamacare legislation, ruling in a 6-3 decision that the Federal government can give out subsidies to its consumers in all states, no matter whether they signed up through the Federal or State based exchanges.

The rate of uninsured Americans dropped below 10 percent for the first time ever. In all, 17.6 million people and climbing have gained coverage.

Other highlights of 2015

1. In this year, 1,125 people killed by police in the U.S.
2. Over five hundred million dollars in global ticket sales made during the opening weekend of Star Wars.
3. Fourteen people were killed in a mass shooting in San Bernardino, California in December, making it the worst since 26 people were killed at Sandy Hook Elementary school in 2012.
4. 100% of Americans won the right to marry their partners after the supreme court ruled that same-sex marriage was legal across the country.
5. In Northern California, wildfires incinerated 61,000 acres, or 95 square miles in September. The wildfires, which are linked to climate

change, displaced 23,000 people and destroyed 14,000 homes in 2 days.

6. Volkswagen recalled 11M diesel vehicles in September after the car manufacturer was embroiled in an emissions scandal.

7. A total of 107 detainees in Guantanamo Bay, Cuba, the U.S. military facility that President Obama pledged in 2009 to close within a year. The American Civil Liberties Union described prison as a failure.

8. 5 to 2 was the final score for the victorious U.S. Women's Soccer Team in their championship match against Japan in July this year. They took home the Women's World Cup, the third time the U.S. has done so since the Cup was established in 1991.

9. A total of 4.4 million Syrian refugees have been registered by the United Nations high commissioner for refugees. Most of them are in Turkey, Lebanon, Jordan and Iraq. Since 2012, the U.S. has accepted 2,174 Syrian refugees, which is roughly 0.0007% of American's total population.

10. 50 Cosby accusers: More than 50 women accused Bill Cosby of sexual assault in 2015. In December, the actor filed a defamation suit against seven of those women.

The Cost of Equality:

Whites and Blacks alike look to the day when segregation will end, and this country will no longer have a well-deserved international reputation for poor race relations. The Supreme Court's decision has committed all citizens, irrevocably, segregation has had certain by-products, certain special privileges which some Blacks may find difficult to relinquish. It is that Black professional, the businessman, and to a lesser extent, the White-collar worker who profit from segregation. These groups in the Black population enjoy certain advantages because they do not have to compete with Whites. The children, too, will be affected. Mildred Faris has observed: "Having won the right to attend school with children of other races, the Black child must now cope with individual insecurities and individual acceptance or rejection.

What was formerly racial rejection having to be dealt with now as rejection of a particular individual or family." Alexander King has paraphrased his personal belief as follows:

"I suppose this is about as opportune that we have these truths to be self-evident that all women and men are created equal."

Never have cause of racial justice been pleaded more cogently than Dr. King. "Free at last, free at last, thank God almighty, we are free at last."

I read in a petition to the Massachusetts Legislature in 1774, a group of slaves in that colony contended that "We have in common with all others, a natural right to our freedoms." By Edgar Toppin.

It is symbolic of the efforts of Black people, then and now, to write a proud record on the pages of history. African Emperors like Mansa Musa rules realms larger than non-Russian Europe, at a time when rapid communication and rapid transportation were lacking.

Black Lives Matter:

The phrase became a common trending hashtag on twitter throughout the year, following events such as the death of 25-year-old Black man, Freddie Gray while in police custody. The death showed yet another light on the continued challenges facing the Black community in the U.S.

Black Lives Matter released a petition calling for a Democratic presidential debate focused on the candidates' policies on racial justice issues.

The Charlie Hebdo Attack:

Two masked gunmen storm the office of Charlie Hebdo, a satirical weekly magazine in Paris, and killed 12 people, including the paper's top editor, Stephanie Charbonnier, several cartoonists and two police officers. Five others were critically injured. The provocative magazine is known for publishing charged cartoons that satirized the prophet Muhammad, most religions, the Pope and several world leaders. French President Francois

Hollard responds to the attack by saying that "France is in shock. "It is the worst terrorist attack in the country since World War II." U.S. President Barack Obama and other world leaders condemned the attack. Eventually, on January 14th Yemen-based Al Qaeda in the Arabian Peninsula claims responsibility for the attack in retaliation for the magazine's caricatures of the Prophet Muhammad.

James A. Goodman stated, "A time as any for me to make clear my attitude on racial prejudice. I am sure I am completely free from it. I want Black and others to get all possible rights of equality because only then will I be able to esteem them, or to loathe them, individually, as I do white people. But at this time, I am still compelled to stand a lot of rudeness, boredom and nonsense from some of my darker brothers simply because some are of specifically offensive individuals, who happen to belong to an abused and injured minority toward who I have an unavoidable sense of guilt. I must personally lick up the memory of all the insults, all the humiliations and all the lynching's that their race has suffered and so I shall never be able to treat them as true equals until all this color inequity stops, once and for all."

The Year 2016

Starting from an unpredictable and tumultuous U.S. presidential election.

A demonstrator protesting the shooting death of Alton Sterling, is detained by law enforcement in Baton Rouge Police department in Louisiana on July 5th. Sterling was shot by police several times while being held on the ground. The incident was on video.

Air Force One carrying U.S. President Barack Obama as his family flies over a neighborhood of Havana, Cuba, on March 20th. Obama was the first president to visit the island nation in 88 years.

Twin blasts at Brussels Airport in Zaventem on March 22nd, as part of coordinated attacks claimed by ISIS militants. Airlines cancelled hundreds of flights and European railways froze links with Brussels after a series of bomb blasts killed 32 people and injured another 300 in the city's airport and a metro train.

Following the 2016 election, President Barack Obama and a bipartisan committee of the U.S. senators called for a CIA investigation into Russian influence in the U.S. election on behalf of Trump, raising red flags among lawmakers concerned about the sanctity of the U.S. voting system and potentially straining relations at the start of Trump's administration.

Black Lives Matter:

Escalating tensions across the country between the Black community and police following the death of Philando Castile, Keith Lamont Scott, Joseph Mann, Gregory Gunn and locally Akai Gurley and Deborah Danner, among others led to a series of riots, protest, and calls for reform from politicians and other activists across the nation through 2016.

On July 11th, police officers were shot, and five of them were killed in Dallas, Texas during protests which was against police brutality. The act was condemned by leaders of the Black Lives Matter movement.

Several days later, Gavin Eugene long, a 29-year Black man from Kansas City Missouri open fire on six police officers, killing 3 of them.

Other Events in 2016

1. Flint, Michigan – Water Crisis:

    January 16th, President Obama signed an emergency order to help Flint, Michigan, address its community's water crisis. The water supply became contaminated after the city switched water systems.

2. Prosecutors: Black bears lured into dog attacks: the individuals arrested face charges of animal cruelty, unlawfully taking of black bears and animal fighting or baiting.

3. Justice Ruth Bader Ginsburg has lung cancer surgery.

4. 8#35; MeToo Movement sparked surge in awareness about sexual harassment study.

5. Ginsburg recovering after cancer removed: the 85-year-old Supreme court Justice is expected to remain in the hospital for a few days.

6. Hepatitis C cases cluster in states hit hard by Opioids.

7. To find the best law firms:

    Methodology Overview Featured Firms.

    1. Fowler Firms

    2. NL – Nutile Law

    3. Carver, Darden, Koreseky, Tessier, Finn, Blossman & Areaux LLC

8. New Year's Eve 2016 is celebrated on Saturday, December 31t.

9. Syrian Civil War was brutal in Syria and was nearing its six-year mark, with no end in sight.

10. Port wine houses have now released their Vintage Port 2016 and although some people would say that it is much too early to drink such a wine now.

The Year 2017

John F. Kennedy is considered one of the greatest American orators of the 20th century. If you have ever listened to a classic Kennedy speech, you would realize it is not only his words, but his delivery that make it memorable. Kennedy's vocal skills, the change of tempo and volume, for example, as well as the visual image of the man helped make some of his speeches forever memorable.

While your next presentation on the company's new quality initiative or re-engineering program may not reach the summit that Kenney sometimes attained, it need not be a boring monologue that sends your audience off to sleep. Instead of settling for a second class talk that will be forgotten almost as soon as you leave the podium, set a higher standard for yourself and your audience will mor likely remember what you said.

2017 is the year of the 3rd Millennium. The 21st Century, and the 8th year of the s010 decade.

1. White Nationalists, Neo-Nazis and members of the "Alt-Right" exchange insults with counter protesters at lee Park during the "Unite the Right Rally" August 12th in Charlottesville, Virginia.

2. Dan Cozey said, "As the new year approaches, it seems like every year is dubbed 'A year like no other.' "but 2017 truly was more dramatic than many other years in recent memory."

3. In the last 12 months, we faced a renewed threat of nuclear war, debated whether to take a knee during the National Anthem and resisted the temptation to look at the sun during the total solar eclipse.

4. From increased tensions with North Korea, to the hurricane season unlike any other, to the bombshell allegations of sexual misconduct in Hollywood and beyond, take a look back at the key moments of 2017, as they were reported by NBC News.

5. Donald Trump was sworn in as the 45th President of the United States January 20th outlining his vision of a new national populism and reiterating the same "America First" mantra that delivered the White House to him during the 2016 election.

6. Bowing to public and congressional pressure, Deputy U.S. Attorney general Rod Rosenstein appointed former FBI, Director Robert Mueller, in May as a special counsel to conduct the investigation into Russian interference in the 2016 presidential campaign.

7. On October 1st, a lone gunman unleased a rapid-fire barrage of bullets down on a crowd of concertgoers from the 32nd floor of the Mandalay Bay resort and Casino in Las Vegas, Nevada, killing 59 people and injuring more than 500 others. It was the deadliest mass shooting in modern American history.

8. Opioids: The White House Council of Economic advisers recently reported that the epidemic's true cost in 2015 was $504 Billion more than six times the most recent estimate.

9. Devastating hurricane season: A hurricane season unlike any other came to a close in December after causing billions of dollars in damages an devastating those who were impacted by Hurricanes Harvey, Irma and Maria when they plowed through Southeast Texas, Florida and the Caribbean.

10. The Total Solar Eclipse: The astronomical phenomenon of the century lived up to the hype. The total solar eclipse shifted across the U.S. in late August, enchanting Americans in small towns and large stadiums from coast to coast. The nation was captivated by the first total solar eclipse to cross the U.S. since 1918.

The Year 2018

A gunman opened fire on Marjory Stoneman Douglas High School in Parkland, Florida, killing 17 students and staff members. The survivors launched a campaign for stricter gun laws.

Coral Springs, Florida, students barricaded themselves inside of classrooms and closets at a high school, while authorities responded to a shooting that they say killed at least 17 people. More than two dozen victims were hospitalized for treatment of various injuries.

On February 20th, students went to the State Capitol in Tallahassee and watched as the Florida House Representatives rejected a bill that would have banned assault weapons. Students strongly criticized the vote.

Other Events:

1. Balangiga Bells finally returns to the PH after 117 years: After more than a century of being away, the Balangiga Bells found their way home to the Philippines. The bells were taken a war bootie by American soldiers from the town of Balangiga in eastern Samar in 1901. They stole it after Filipino troops killed 48 American soldiers as revenge for forcing the locals to work in their camps.

A Filipino official stated that the bells were returned to the country thanks to the efforts of two American veteran organizations, and not through the work of the Duterte Administration.

2. Worcester, Massachusetts: Family Health Center of Worcester, Inc. was awarded with a $106,405 grant from the U.S. Department of Health and Human services/Health Resources and Services Administration (HRSA) for achieving a high level of quality performance. In 2017, including recognition as a national quality leader (Gold Award) in as a health center quality leader (Silver Award) nationally, HRSA awarded $125 Million to 1,352 community health centers across the U.S. for quality improvement.

3. The Red Sox Showcase bring mini-Fenway Park to Worcester, August 2018. It would be great to get to Fenway Park to see the surging Boston Red Sox, but if you cannot get there, don't worry, Fenway Park is coming to Worcester on Friday. The Red sox Showcase is a transportable Fenway Park featuring an interactive baseball program that will let children and families get into the game, and experience baseball like the pros. Activities will include a batting cage, "The Red sox virtual reality experience", Pitching accuracy stations, steal 2nd base challenge and a green monster selfie station.

4. Argania: Argania is a genius of flowering plants containing the sole species Argania spinosa, known as argan, a tree endemic to the calcareous semidesert sous valley of Southwest Morocco. Argan trees grow to 8-10 M high and live up to approximately 200 years to 450 years. Goats feed on an Argan tree. In Essaouira, Morocco, there is something mighty tasty ab out the fruit and leaves of an Argan tree, at least if you agree, a goat living in the arid landscape of Western Morocco. Once the goats finish plucking treats from the lower hanging branches, these skilled climbers scramble their way up and across higher branches looking for more. The goats delight tourists, but they are rather a mixed bag for the Argan trees themselves. The goat's digestive system. The Argan tree is quite a thorny evergreen that may not come into full production until it is 40-60 years old.

5. Shares of Exxon Mobil declined a painful 18.5% in 2018 according to data provided by S&P Global Market Intelligence. Fellow international energy giant Chevron (NYSE: CVX) lost 13.1% of its value. The pain, meanwhile, was not confined to U.S. based companies. Royal Dutch Shell (NYSE: PTR), one of the largest energy players in China, were both down around 12% latter part of this particular year. Other big names took hits too, including BP (British Petroleum) and total, though their declines were more modest at less than 10%.

It is never pleasing to see a stock you own have a down year. But sometimes the ups and downs are simply to be expected. That is particularly the case with energy companies like Exxon, Chevron, Shell and Petro-China.

6. Energy Stocks for Year 2018: the more-than-doubling of crude oil prices over the past couple of years has been a difficult rally to trust energy companies still are not exactly highly disciplined outfits despite the pain of overproduction they inflicted on themselves back in 2014. On the other hand, the bears have had every opportunity to upend the rally but have been unable to do so. Perhaps a price of more than $60 per barrel really is the "New normal" for the energy market. At the very least, investors would be wise to expect that not investing in energy stock could be riskier than being in them for the foreseeable future.

7. A longer life and healthier body: just from sitting on your couch you may experience weight gain, fatigue, foggy thinking and achy joints. These are the hallmarks of what we call "aging". But according to a doctor, that may be about to change. "Every year we get older, but what this discovery means is, we don't have to feel older, and we don't have to look older, "says Dr. Rand McClain, one of the top regenerative medicine specialists in Los Angeles. Dr. McClain's research has to do with the science of telomeres – the tiny "caps" that protect the DNA in our cells. Research now shows these caps get shorter and shorter as we age, leading to a host of ailments including weight

gain, fatigue, body aches and cognitive issues. Research at Harvard shows shorter telomeres are associated with cardiovascular disease and even cancer.

Dr. Rand McClain is an expert in the areas of anti-aging medicine and rejuvenation. He is on the cusp on new approaches to improving life quality through proper nutrition, and hormone balancing. His procedures and therapies are based on science and proven personally through his own practice. Therapies he promotes include:

Intramuscular, oral and IV nutrition and supplement therapy, platelet-rich plasma therapy, corticosteroid injections, therapeutic exercise activity and bioidentical hormone replacement therapy. Is client list extend from celebrities' world class athletes to housewives.

Top News Categories through Alexa Ranking:

Nowadays, most of the people prefer the online websites to read the latest news rather than a newspaper. There was a time when everyone needed to wait for a newspaper in the early morning, but now, in this technological world, you do not need to wait for a newspaper. You can read the latest news on your mobile phone, tablet, PC or laptop.

1. Google News is the most famous news site. Basically, it is a new aggregator and app. Open news google.com to get the latest news. You can read news about all categories. Also, you can read a country wide news and world news and can select your country's edition for country-specific news.

2. Yahoo news is another popular news aggregator and website. You can get the latest news of every category from Yahoo News. Yahoo News' articles come from other news services like ABC News, CNN News and BBC News.

3. ISIS' News frontier: CNN News (cable news network) is a famous and popular international news website. CNN is basically an Amer-

ican news channel and is also a famous news website in all around the world. Alexa ranking is 103.

4. BBC News (British Broadcast Company) is popular all over the world. Everyone knows about the BBC. Well, the news website of BBC is also popular. The Alexa rank of BBC News is 105. US rank is 68.

5. The first newspaper of the New York times was published in 1851. But now the Times has been changed. Most users read the news online. S, New York Times News website is useful for those users.

Other News Outlet listed below:

   a. Washington Post – A popular world newspaper.

   b. India Times – is an Indian website.

   c. Huffington Post – most categories like technology, entertainment, business, lifestyle, politics and local news.

   d. Fox News – is a news channel own by Fox Entertainment group. (The Alexa Rank of Fox News is 280).

   e. USA Today – is a news website for USA readers and is also popular in many countries. (The Alexa Rank of USA Today is 533)

   f. The Wall Street Journal – is an American International Newspaper.

   g. NBC News – is famous in all the world for its latest news. (The Alexa Rank of NBC News is 828, US traffic Rank is 209).

   h. ABC News (America Broadcasting Company) – is the best for international news.

The Alexa Rank is a global ranking system that ranks millions of websites in order of popularity.

It is calculated by looking at the estimated average daily unique visitors and number of pageviews for a given the site over the last 3 months. The lower your Alexa rank, the more popular the website is.

Interesting Story: Bear Brook

The true crime genre is crowded with podcast, but "Bear Brook", from New Hampshire Public Radio (NHPR) stands out for its ambition, complexity and thoughtful tone. The series centers on a cold case from 1985, involving four bodies found in a barrel near Bear Brook State Park, in Allenstown, New Hampshire. Until recently, no one knew who the victims were or who had killed them, and the case mystified locals and investigators for decades. Bear Brook is not far from NHPR's studios and the young NHPR beat reporter, Jason Moon, worked on the series for three years. "Something to when I wasn't sitting at a town-hall meeting or covering the state legislature," he says in episode 1. With remarkable sensitivity and knack for scene setting, Moon guides us through thicket of grisly story lines spanning several decades, characters, aliases and states, in narrative that culminates in an investigator's discovery of a revolutionary, controversial DNA technique, which both solved the case of the Golden State Killer and brings Bear Brook ever closer to resolution.

Things to think about:

It is helpful to have well thought out plans in place, so you are a more informed person. It is a strategy it legitimate, that people will recognize. I have lived by this principal all my life. Do not speak for people, advise people, if your intellect share in the conversation. A discussion will be not whether they exist but how they exist. For example, economy today seems out of control, et us search for economic explanations and education. Economic goals require considerably more actions, less talk. To provide facts, like truism over procrastination, performance results is an advancement results – the public is tired of surreptitious by taking away items and facts and making assumptions. Remember more than ever the middle-class is now altruistic.

For example: CN Fortune the Boston Globe; Buford, GA – how 2 math grads are disrupting the auto insurance industry.

Atlanta, Georgia with over 260 million licensed drivers in the U.S. it is no wonder this startup is taking off and saving people money for free!!

Are you aware that you could receive a large discount by using this new startup's service in addition, if you live in certain zip codes, you may get extremely low rates? For a long time, there was no comparing quotes from all these huge car insurance companies. You had to check one site, then jump to another and enter all your information all over again. Drivers were stuck doing all the work to save money. Now, all that is changing. Thanks to this new startup "Every Quote", the information you need to help save can be found in one place. Every quote is not an insurer, but a comparison-shopping marketplace. Featured in the INC 5000 list as one of the fastest growing companies for 2017, it is not a question that customers are finding what they are looking for…lower quotes.

What exactly do you need? Here is one easy rule to follow. You must compare quotes. Do not even consider buying car insurance without doing this first. After all the results we came across, we just could not believe how many drivers have been overpaying. And with free services like Ever Quote, comparing quotes today so that you are not accidentally costing yourself money is a breeze.

Drivers do not always realize that they maybe overpaying. Fortunately, millions of smart drivers have used Ever Quote's free service to save hundreds on their insurance bills.

It is no wonder that with so many drivers saving money, Ever Quote is gaining momentum. Ever Quote is an efficient source that tries to give consumers the lowest rates with tools you can trust. Just imagine what you can do with the money you save!

Once you are on the website, you put in your zip code, and driver's information then you can start to compare all your quotes.

More Events:

Afghanistan. UN says record number of civilians killed in 2018. Increase in ISIS suicide bombings and U.S.-led airstrikes blamed for nearly 4,000 deaths. In its annual report published on during this time, the U.N assistance mission in Afghanistan (UNAMR) said 3,804 civilians were killed in 2018, the highest toll since it began compiling figures in 2009. Another 7,189 were wounded.

The UNAMA report said 2018 witnessed the highest number of civilian casualties ever recorded from suicide attacks and aerial operations. According to the report, 63 percent of all civilian casualties were caused by militants with the Taliban being blamed for 37 percent of the dead and wounded, the Islamic State, a militant group, for 20 percent and other antigovernment groups for 6 percent.

The Afghan government and its U.S. and NATO allies were blamed for 24 percent of the dead and wounded civilians, many of them killed in increased air strikes carried out mostly by international forces.

For the first time since 2009, UNAMA recorded more than 1,000 civilian casualties from aerial operations," the report said.

The U.S. military said it carried out 6,823 sorties last year in which munitions were fired, the highest number in the last six years. Deeply disturbing!

UNAMA said women and children comprised almost two-thirds of all civilian casualties from aerial operations.

The uptick in violence in 2018 also coincided with a significant increase in the number of deaths caused by the "deliberate targeting of civilians," according to the report, mostly stemming from suicide attacks by the Taliban or the ISIS group.

At least 65 suicide attacks were recorded in 2018, the majority hitting the capital Kabul. The report said the Taliban was responsible for 1,715 civilian casualties in 2018 compared to 916 in 2017, while the ISIS group killed or wounded 2,181 civilians last year (2017) the highest number ever recorded for the militant groups.

The report's release comes a day before U.S. and Taliban negotiators hold another round of peace talk in Qatar aimed at ending the 17-year conflict.

U.S. Peace envoy Zalmay Khalilzad has held a series of direct talks with Taliban negotiators across the Middle East in recent months, raising the prospect of peace.

Tadamichi Yamamoto, the head of the UN mission in Afghanistan, called the spiraling number of civilian casualties "deeply disturbing and wholly unacceptable."

"It is time to put an end to this human misery and tragedy," said Yamamoto. "The best way to halt the killings and maiming of civilians is to stop the fighting." (Information from The Insider).

Here are some news stories that captivated me this year:

1. The wedding of Prince Harry and Meghan Markle captivated the world.

2. Twelve boys and their soccer coach got stranded in a cave in Thailand, and the world rallied to their rescue.

3. Facebook's Cambridge Analytica scandal revealed that more than 50 million people's personal information was compromised for "research."

4. Kim Jong Un announced that North Korea will denuclearize the net neutrality debate came to a head, and the FCC's rules were repealed, putting the control back in the internet's hands. (The Insider).

5. House Minority Leader Nancy Pelosi and Senator Charles Schumer at a press conference advocating for net neutrality.

6. Testimony in the Brett Kavanaugh hearings, when Dr. Christine Blasey Ford gave her testimony during the Senate Judiciary Committee hearings regarding her sexual assault allegations against Supreme Court Nominee Brett Kavanaugh. Women with similar stories worldwide united.

7. Puerto Rico was left without electricity for 11 months and the world came together to help in the wake of Hurricane Maria.

8. The Castro family's more than 50-year reign over Cuba came to an end with the election of Miguel Diaz-Canel.

9. This year Iraqi voters held their first election since driving out the Islamic State (aka ISIS) in 2017 after the Iraqi Civil War. It was a milestone election for the country, and Iraqis were given the power to decide their future with the potential to shift the balance of power and mend divisions between ethnic groups.

Additional through provoking issues:

1. The world's richest self-made women: The women doing it for themselves while men continue to dominate the top of the world's rich list, an increasing number of women are scaling the ranks. According to Forbes, billionaire rankings with many of them making their fortunes themselves.

2. The social studies classroom – Immigration and xenophobia are themes that run through U.S. history. This image accompanies an op-ed detail how Italian immigrants were once victims of racism, hatred and abuse. (Related article – Emiliano Ponzi)

3. Why do we insist that students study history? Perhaps because the study of history promotes critical thinking, creates a shared cultural literacy or encourages responsible citizenship. Certainly, one of the most important reasons is because history continues to matter. (Michael Gonchar, New York Times)

4. Why has North Korea developed a nuclear arsenal that threatens the United States? Why are thousands of Hondurans camped out on the southern border of the United States? Why have many athletes decided to kneel during the National Anthem? To answer any of these questions, or the myriad others posed by the news everyday – students will need to understand what happened in the past.

5. In this teaching resource, we suggest different methods teachers can use to easily facilitate these connections. Each method is illustrated with two examples, one from global history and another from the United States history and each end with a classroom challenge. The

goal is to help this kind of thinking become a habit of mind for your students.

6. To encourage students, they ran a contest in 2018 from December 6 to January 21st that invited any teenage anywhere in the world to link a topic learned in school this semester with something in the news. The winners of the former year's contest came up with ideas such as comparing the Chinese Exclusion Act to President Trump's ban of citizens from seven predominately Muslim countries.

7. United States. How much power should the president have? That is a question or society is debating today. And since Donald J. Trump was elected, a flurry of executive orders, court rulings, confirmation hearings and tussles with the press have made the questions more relevant than ever.

8. Is democracy at risk? A lesson plan for U.S. and Global History classes:

- Analyzing the relationship between the press and the President.
- Teaching and learning about governmental checks and balances and the
- Trump administration.
- (Worlds Within the Atom, by John Boslough)

The White House issues a simple statement this year (2018) as hundreds of thousands of people descended on Washington D.C., New York and cities around the country and world to protest gun violence at "March for Our Lives Rallies." Mr. Trump is at his club in Mar-a-largo in Palm Beach, Florida this weekend about 40 miles from the Parkland High School where 17 people were killed the month before.

The president went to his golf club in the area on the Saturday of the protest, but, like usual, White House aides did not tell the press pool what Mr. Trump was doing there. As of that afternoon, Mr. Trump has yet to issue any comments about the rallies from his Twitter account.

White House press secretary, Lindsay Walters said they "applaud the many courageous young Americans", speaking out Saturday, pointing to what Mr. Trump has done to address gun violence. The Omnibus Spending Bill Mr. Trump signed Friday afternoon – after threatening to veto it, included provisions to strengthen the background check system and fund DOJ (Department of Justice) resources for stopping school threats.

On Friday, Mr. Trump and Attorney General Jeff Sessions also announced the new federal rule to ban pump stocks, a device used in last year's Las Vegas shooting that allows legal guns to function like automatic weapons. "We applaud the many courageous young Americans exercising their First Amendment rights today," Walters said. "Keeping our children safe is a top priority of the president which is why he urged Congress to pass the Fix Nics and stop School Violence Acts and signed them into law. Additionally, on Friday, the Department of Justice issued the rule to ban bump stocks following through on the president's commitment to ban devices that turn legal weapons into illegal machine guns."

Mr. Trump has said he wants to be "very strong" on background checks, arm teachers and other campus officials, and perhaps raise the age for purchasing some guns from 18 t0 21.

But raising the age for gun purchases has little support from Republicans, who control both the House and the Senate. The president has said some Republicans are petrified of the National Rifle Association but maintains that the leaders of the NRA are "great people." (CBS News)

A Free Man Behind Enemy Lines; He Built 100 Bridges in the Future Confederacy:

The covered bridge trembles as a Lexus rolls through, past one beam charred by fire, past several others warped by a flood. The driver goes slowly, going gingerly through pale sunlight that rises from cracks in the floor and descends from bullet holes in the roof. Tires click and pop on pine. First came the covered wagons, then the model T. Fords, and now this white Lexus SUV on a clear Saturday morning driven by a woman who wants to see the bridge.

They are 54.2 miles South of Atlanta, the woman and the bridge, with a rust color creek whispering beneath them and birds singing in the trees overhead. She might be 50. The Red Oak Creek covered bridge might by 175 in age. It has stood here in Meriwether County for some 63,000 days, outlasting more than 30 presidents, surviving high water and shotgun blasts and pocketknives and carpenter bees and heat and cold and rain and snow and that august humidity that makes the air a stale bath. The Lexus emerges from inside the bridge. "I feel sacrilegious just driving over it," the woman said through her open windows to no one and drives over it again. The bride's longevity is nearly as astounding as the story of its builder, Horace King, part Black, and part White, part Catawba Indian, Square jaw, flinty gaze, a man so far ahead of his time that he wore a soul patch 60 years before anyone heard of Jazz.

King was born into slavery in South Carolina in 1807. He and his master, John Godwin, learned a sophisticated b ridge-building technique called the "Town lattice-truss" and King showed so much talent for the work, that Godwin essentially made him a partner. The two men traveled around the Antebellum South, helping expand its infrastructure to the West. They built a bridge across the Chattahoochee River that linked Columbus to Alabama, and when a flood washed it away, they got a contract to build it again. Godwin, under pressure to finish the job quickly, told king that if they met their deadline, he would let him free.

They finished the bridge on time, and though it took an act of the Alabama legislature, Godwin kept his word. Godwin dies in 1859. King carried on without him, a free man behind enemy lines, building more than 100 bridges in what would soon become the Confederate States of America. He built a rolling mill, for the Confederate Navy. It was a strange position, helping the slave holder fight their war and even stranger when the Army of liberators began destroying his work.

One by one, Kings bridges fell at the Battle of Moore's bridges in Carroll County in 184, retreating Union soldiers set fire to a 480-foot span across the Chattahoochee. They went on to burn Atlanta in this pre-telephone era, a week after General Lee's surrender, Union Cavalry made a needless raid on Fort Tyler, at West Point. Twenty-six men died, and the Union burned King's bridge. King rebuild the bridge in Carroll county after the war, but a flood swept it away in 1881. Five years later, a few years before King's death, another flood destroyed his bridge in Wetumpka, Alabama. Wooden covered bridges went out of style, replaced by concrete and steel, and some fell apart from neglect. Officials from Callaway Gardens preserved a King bridge from Troup County that would have been put underwater by the West Point Dam. In Meriwether County in 1985, someone torched the bridge over White Oak Creek.

Covered bridges in Georgia dwindled from more than 250. Of all the bridges that king built in Georgia, only one remains in use, and if Bruce O'Neal has his way, it will never fall.

("Bridge at Red Oak Creek" written by Thomas Lake)

My thoughts: Equivocally is capable of interpretations, cryptic, evasive, ambiguous. Cryptic. A meaning that is mysterious or obscure.

When one thing is predicated of another, all that which predicate will be predicable also of the subject, thus, "man" is predicated of the individual man; but animal is predicated of man – it will therefore be predicable of the individual man also: for individual man is both "man" and "animal."

"Faces of Africa" by Carol Beckwith and Angela Fisher (thirty years of photography)

Africa's rich and astonishingly diverse cultural traditions come alive in this book.

The genesis of "Faces of Africa" took place in the great rift valley of Kenya, where Donald Young, Barney Wan and Kuki Galtmann gathers to explore with Beckwith and Fisher. The underlying themes that define traditional African life with unflagging energy and dedication, Donald Young went on to work with the authors in Nairobi and later in London, helping them to develop visual themes and craft their chapter introductions. Donald's understanding of traditional African life, after 30 years in Africa as a historian and Safari guide, coupled with his belief in Beckwith and Fisher's work has made him an invaluable partner in the creation of "Faces of Africa."

A spiritual message:

Believing in God is easier than believing in others. If you have deeply rooted faith, loving, healing with truth, God always takes care of us, when we believe in Him. I hope you will have the courage to trust vibrantly in His charismatic personality. Gave we found ourselves in exoteric times and no one to turn to and insights leads to God's wisdom? Being prepared and wise with wisdom, produces the hope we have in Jesus.

Hope in the spiritual realm allows you to excel beyond existence circumstances. It is amazing what we can endure when we have Jesus in our hearts but after time passes, we can renew and see God's kindness through our confusion to something good.

I read a quotation by Martin Luther King, Jr., "Take the first step in faith. You do not have to see the whole staircase, just take the first step."

God, I think, speaks to all of us, through His spirit, learn to be quiet so you can recognize when it happens. His message is spiritually compendium.

Believing Integrity: Having the quality of being honest and having strong moral principles, moral uprightness is a gift from God.

The main purpose how God's plan for educating mankind, and women kind, they must read the Bible from Genesis to Revelation.

By reading the Bible you will understand this book included Northeastern part of Africa and Southwestern Asia. Archaeologists who studied the past by digging ruins that led them to the great flood in Mesopotamia, it caused massive conditions of clay and mud, but Noah is saved so he was part of the plan to start the human race all over.

The Year 2019

RECONSTRUCTION:

Introducing a new dimension to strategic planning. Complicity means "the state of being an accomplice as in wrongdoing." My primary concern. To improve the ability to differentiate by gaining control over the good people to give the poor a free education on the principles of completing a trade school or college education. Why? To pursue approaches dictated by its professional orientation of those in charge. It will soon be apparent reflecting and to guide people to gain strategy for articulation key factors to eliminate poverty and to gain industry opportunities for the poor white or black males or females.

Let us eliminate the rule that a child can quit school at age 16. This proposal will also translate into less crime, it will give industry a monetary return because more of our citizens will be more educated and can place this country on a path that will eventually eliminate poverty. I cannot understand why Germany's strategy for a college education for everyone, a free implementable new set of rules cannot be duplicated.

Individuals that are incarcerated should be educated, complete college or master a trade before they can be released into society. People who have learned a skill or higher learning are more self-sustaining and commit less crime. Currently, the poor are growing at an alarming rate as more middle-class citizens are joining the poor ranks. This matter about poverty, race relations, should be a thing of the past.

Remember, college is for everyone not just for the rich.

Spiritual Reflections:

The environment today, being prepared and equipped with truth in Jesus I ask my mind to wade into areas that life is closing in on us with darkened feeling as I observe the burdens of life, and it is never easy. I pray every day and I hope Jesus will show His face and assert a message so man can see Him entirely. The proof of love is trust.

Serving others is good for the soul. Volunteering is the best way to honor a man or woman who dedicated his or her life to serving others. On this year of esoteric behavior in this country and the world, this technique for analyzing human behavior, it is not complicated, if you create your own legacy by giving back in your community. Understanding the nature of our biblical commitment, I believe that all over the world a straightforward guide to what religion is and applied it every day.

Equality in the world:

The reader will note that equality is not one of the omissions may derive entirely from the degree of arbitrariness that admittedly is involved in constructing for the light they throw on equality, there has always been suspicion that equality places lies in mathematical order. It has been historically a subject of justice of democracy.

The issue of equality as it applies to black people and poor whites.

1. Equality before the law
2. Equality of honor
3. Equality of political rights
4. Equality of votes or suffrage
5. Equality of tax tribute

In the beginnings of history, our ancestors succeeded in developing a human race

advancement. The development of a working economy, a language that makes it easier

to communicate and fair political developments, and the evolution of human society. We

have noticed over the years the closing of the racial gap.

Current Events in 2020:

For current event summaries that we can trust, they almost always in upon captivating images and news briefs about critical discoveries, technology breakthroughs and news events organized chronologically. In global independent news, Democracy Now, produces a daily, global independent news hour hosted by award-winning journalists Amy Goodman and Juan Gonzalez. Their reporting includes breaking daily news headlines and in-depth interviews with people on the phonelines of the world's most pressing issues. On Democracy Now, you'll hear a diversity of voices speaking for themselves, providing a unique and sometimes provocative perspective on global events.

Democracy Now and Senator Kamala Harris made me aware that companies with gender pay gap from the 2020 campaign trails, California senator Kamala Harris announced her proposal of close the gender pay gap that will hold companies liable if they fail to introduce an equal pay measure.

The plan would require all companies with a 100 or more employees to earn equal pay certification "by proving they pay men and women the same for doing work of the same value, or else be fines 1% of their profits for every 1% wage gap. It would also force corporations to report the share of women in leadership positions, bar them from asking about prior salary history and prohibit them from using forced arbitration to handle pay discrimination claims.

Harris has deemed her plan a "first-ever" national priority on closing that pay gap, but it does have some close peers. It is similar to an Obama-era rule that required employers of 100-plus workers to report pay data by race and gender (you might recall that the Trump administration tried to revoke the rule for being too "burdensome" to business, but a judge rejected that rationale in March of this year a ruling the administration is now appealing).

But Harris' plan adds a punitive layer in the form of the fine, introducing what could be a powerful stick to the equation. That aligns her proposal with initiatives passed in Iceland and France, where gender pay gap reporting is accompanies by financial penalties. And that contrasts her idea with the approach taken in the United Kingdom where forms don't face fines for the gender pay gaps they report; the idea being that naming and shaming is enough of a motivator.

Harris is already playing up the threat her plan will improve at a rally that previewed the announcement she made. She said, "Her measure will hold corporations accountable for transparency and closing that gap. There will be penalties if they don't," she said to applause.

The fine certainly adds teeth to the initiative, plus it is a revenue stream. Her campaign estimates it will generate $180 billion in the first decade, which will, in turn, help fund a paid family and medical leave plan that Senator Kirsten Gillibrand has introduced, and Harris has backed. But at the same time, the fine is, essentially, a new tax on business, which means implementing the plan in its entirety would require congressional support.

This is important since the proposal is likely to face opposition from Republicans. "We don't need to strap new regulations, burdens or fines on businesses to create opportunities for women, and President Trump's economic record is testament to that," a spokeswoman for the Republican National Committee said in response to the idea.

But on her side, Harris has that pesky 20% pay gap, which is even worse for Black and Latina women and research that says that when companies are required to disclose their pay data, their gender gaps shrink. (Claire Zillman, Senior Editor; Fortune Magazine)

My thoughts:

It seems to me that the modern world is displaying, from great current events of history, are carrying the world away from the monolithic towards a pluralist idea.

Additional Events of the year:
President Trump cited President Andrew Jackson as his favorite president. This was Trump speaking on NBC in 2016.

Andrew Jackson was a slave holder who, in 1830, signed the Indian Removal Act, which forced 16,000 Native Americans from their lands in what became known as the Trail of Tears. Note: Andrew Jackson no longer represents values that Americans say they celebrate and fight for.

Harriet Tubman was about 27 years old in 1849 and her enslaver had died and left his family deeply in debt and in order to pay those debts, they were going to sell Tubman and her family. So, she decided she would take her chances by running away and taking her own liberty, which she did do with the help of black and white underground Railroad Operators, and she made her way to Philadelphia.

But when she arrived there, she was nominally free, but freedom was not what she expected it to be, because everyone she loved was in Maryland, and they were enslaved. Therefore, she was determined that she would go back and rescue them. And for over 10 years, she returned 13 times to bring away all of family members and people that she loved.

When the Civil War started, her mission was to make sure that all people were liberated, and she brought her battle against the South with the United States Army and became a spy and a scout. And she was a remarkably successful scout and greatly admired by Civil War Union generals and officers and soldiers alike.

Equality:

Equality of opportunity is this generalized sense describes an ideal of a good society: a society in which each man is free and able to seek the good life as he sees it and in which all men are equal inasmuch as all have an equal opportunity to engage in the pursuit of their own happiness. All other equalities serve this equality as a means since legal, political, economic, or social equality is viewed merely as a means for achieving that condition in which each man can live as he wants to live. Equality of opportunity understood in this way is the supreme object of policy.

The 3 positions compared from the summary view, we have obtained of the basic theories regarding the justification of equality, we can now see how they stand with respect to one another.

The "formalist position" is clearly the simplest of the three. If the formalist proponents are right in their claim, no justification is needed for the rule of equal treatment, nor is there any need to bother about its consequences.

Th "Pragmatist position" is more complex than the formalist position, but simpler than the "Naturalist Position." If the pragmatist authors are right, the rule for equal treatment is justified by its consequences, and any further question concerns, not the rule, but those consequences and whether they are good, and weather equal treatment does in fact lead to them.

The "Naturalist Position" is the most complex of the three. If its proponents are right, the prior equality rooted in the nature of man not only justified the rule for equal treatment but also explains why the consequences follow from observance of the rule as well as why they are judged to be good: the free pursuit of happiness corresponds to a right judged to be good. The free pursuit of happiness corresponds to a right based on man's nature.

It should also be noted that more complex positions include and do not deny the assertion of the simpler. Both the naturalist and pragmatist authors would admit the formalist assertion that equal treatment is a moral rule, but they would also claim that it involves something more than this. So too, the naturalist authors would agree with the proponents of the pragmatist position that equal treatment leads to certain consequences, that are good. But they go further than this and assert also that both rule and the consequences, are based on a prior equality, the equality of men as men.

Government by discussion is essentially a free and democratic society. Any form of government depends upon discussion, at least among its leaders, as a means of determining policy. But a democratic government differs from others to the extent to which it must resort to discussion. A large and important part of the business of governing is carried on in deliberative assemblies that are open to the public. In addition, the government must periodically render an account to the people whom it serves. It must then engage in discussion which the nation at large.

There are many subjects of political discussion, but all tend to fall into one of their general groups accordingly as the object of concern is primarily a person, a policy or a principle. The first of these subjects needs no explanation. Discussion in any election year turns upon the persons seeking to win election to political office. Candidates, however, expound policies, that it, they draw up plans and outline undertakings to meet special needs and solve problems. But, beyond these, political discussion also not infrequently involves questions of principle and general ideas regarding the ends and basic means of government. Politics then becomes most completely concerned with ideas as such although it sounds paradoxical, especially in an election year, it is nonetheless true that ideas, and not persons or policies, constitute the most important subject of political discussion. Compared with ideas, person and policies are transcend and short-lived, sine discussion of them is limited to the life of the candidate or the urgency of the problem for which the policy is discussion of the ideas involved in the problems of government grows proliferates with their application to new and changing conditions. Even a relatively new idea upon the political scene, such as the ideal of political and social equality for all, has a long history of discussion behind it.

It is with ideas in this, sense of the word that our symposium is concern. The participants were invited to reflect freely upon the role of ideas in politics. However, wince this is the year of the presidential election, we have intentionally focused attention upon politics in the United States. All four contributors have long experience in dealing with the subject of the symposium. Two of them have been associated with the academic profession. Senator Eugene McCarthy was a professor of sociology before he entered politics, and his books have expounded and analyzed political ideas as well as advocated policies. Mr. Arthur Schlesinger Jr. is the Albert Schweitzer professor of the humanities at City College, New York, and is well known for his books on American politics. Yet he, like Mr. Theodore Sorensen, has also been an "idea man" in the field of practical politics. Both having served as special assistants to the late President Kennedy. The fourth participant, Mr. Richard.

H Revere, long an observer of the political scene, is known or his penetrating and learned commentary upon, it, especially as seen from Washington.

These essays were all written before President Johnson's announcement that he would not be a candidate for reelection and of course, before subsequent events.

Two other contributions to this year's volume also bear upon the subject of the symposium, although, they do not appear in it. The first of these is the analysis by Professor John Plamenatz, Serbian political philosopher, of some recent American studies of democracy, in the course which he has occasion to comment on the place and function of ideas in the democratic process. The other, and in fact the longest essay on the subject in this book is the fifth chapter of Walter Bagehot's "Physics and Politics", reprinted in part four; Entitled "Discussion, Public Opinion, and the Meaning of Parliamentary Government", it is an examination of ideas in the advancement of human progress. Bagehot was an English journalist.

(Thank you to – The Enlighten Story Ideas and Politics by William Benton, politician)

Frederick Douglass:

Amy Goodman, American broadcast journalist, covered a piece on Frederick Douglass.

In this special broadcast she echoed the words of Douglass born into slavery around 1818 and He became a key leader of the abolitionist movement. On July 5th, 1852, in Rochester, New York, he gave one of his most famous speeches, "What to the slave is the fourth of July?" He was addressing Rochester ladies' anti-slavery society.

This same year on Frederick Douglass was asked to speak in celebration of the 4th of July. He said, "Fellow citizens, pardon, me, allow me to ask, why am I called upon to speak here today? What have I, or those I represent, to do with your national independence? Are the great principles of political freedom and the natural justice, embodied in that declaration of independence, extended to us? And am I, therefore, called upon to bring our humble offering to the national alter and to confess the benefits and express devout gratitude for the blessings resulting from your independence to us?"

"I am not included within the pale of the glorious anniversary! Your high independence only reveals the immeasurable distance between us. The blessing in which you this day rejoiced in common. The rich inheritance of justice, liberty, prosperity, and independence bequeathed by your fathers is shared by you, not by me. This sunlight that brought life and healing to you brought stripes and death to me. This fourth of July is yours, not mine. You may rejoice, I must mourn. To bring to drag a man in fetters into the rand illuminated temple of liberty and call upon him to join you in joyous anthems, were inhuman mockery and sacrilegious iron do you mean, citizens, to mock me, by asking me to speak today?

"What, to the American slave is your fourth of July? I answer. A day that revels to him, more than all other days of the year, the injustice and cruelty in which he is a constant victim. To him, your celebration I a sham; your boasted liberty, an unholy license, your national greatness, swelling vanity; your sounds of rejoicing and empty and heartless, your denunciation of tyrants brass fronted impudence; your shouts of liberty and equality, hollow mockery, your prayers and hymns, your sermons and thanksgivings, with all your religious shade and solemnity are, to him, mere bombast, fraud, deception, impiety, and hypocrisy – a thin veil to cover up crimes that would disgrace a nation f savages. There is not a nation of the earth, guilty of practices more shocking and bloodier than are the people of these United States at this very hour."

Armageddon

Armageddon is defined in the dictionary as "A final battle between the forces of good and evil." The world today from my narrative that all countries and talking to each other maybe not agreeing with each, but equanimity is in play. The foundation of revolutionary changes in place it's like a winter garden, no longer a storm. Yet skepticism despite the conditions favoring the influence of the intellectual thought. Expiration of the world racist remarks are ending in the world. Note, periodically the government must render an account to its citizens of this nation. Political discussion should involve policies, urgency that proliferates with changing conditions. The purpose of government is to, from a perfect union, equality and housing education, and employment has further progress. Proclamation of ideals achieve by good politician. The modern campaigns extend itself a new elimination of poverty. The extend publicize research that has a growing need for honesty.

Interpretations that are favoring the shaping of the future's political arena, few politicians on both parties execute eagerly are said to get elected or reelected at any cost, have new ideas on issues and leaving out today's economy.

Political leaders today who have heated issues are intellectually arrogant and they leave no judgement for trust. Political ideas today, I see no value in policies thinking an abstract resolution, to describe a concepts immortality. Maybe the concept of making peace internationally is on track, with God's, would advocate. But the persons that thinks uses it to mean that the product of man's thinking is abstract. I think political ideas should be left to the people that vote rather than political people who are doctrine in by generally indifferent contradiction on a platform. This statement of ordinary intelligence that I advocate matters related to showing compassion for all God's children regardless of their skin color.

The constitution of the United States: We the people of the United States in order to form a more perfect union, establish justice, ensure domestic tranquility, provide for the common defense, promoted the general welfare and secure the blessings of liberty to ourselves and our posterity, do ordain and establish this constitution for the United States of America.

My goal is to fix the standard of weights and measures – according to what is disciplined by Congress.

No person, only a natural born American citizen can become president of the United States.

Congress shall have the power to make all rules and regulations.

Citizens of the United States cannot be denied the right to vote.

While mainstream audiences see board games about the brutalization of entire peoples as no more than a history lesson that entertains. I am no stranger to racism: I overheard slurs towards other minority students in the hallways and bathrooms of my high school, I often wonder is such language is directed towards me when I am not within earshot. Products like racist board games bring this sentiment into the light and create pride around defending it. Whether fans realize it or not, buy playing the fame, they legitimize the white supremacists' fantasy of dominating savage peoples – peoples with rich cultures whose history is still a traumatic memory.

The sad reality is minorities cannot afford to forget racism. We must continually remind everyone of who we are, so they do not imagine us as outsiders. As aliens. As savages. If society never meet anyone like us, our identities grow distant, and it becomes easier for us to be dehumanized. It should not be our responsibility to fight implicit bias but instances of latent racism like the board games, tell me that it still is.

(Article from the New York Times)

A spiritual message:

A biblical adventure, it means to know God that is the greatest thing when you search for Him and realize the comfort His message will being to your life, but God demonstrates His own love toward us.

"In Him we have redemption through His blood, the forgiveness of sins, according to the riches of His grace." – Ephesians 1:7.

The Holy Spirit will come upon you and the power of the Highest will overshadow you, because of the one who will be born will be called the son of God for with God nothing will be impossible.

"For prophecy never had its origin in the human will, but prophets, though human, spoke from God as they were carried along by the Holy Spirit." 2 Peter 1:21.

"All Scripture is given by inspiration of God, and is profitable for doctrine, for instruction in righteousness." 2 Timothy 3:16.

"We are mistaken, not knowing the Scriptures nor the power of God." Matthew 22:29

"For it is the God who commanded light to shine out of darkness who has shone in our hearts to give the light of the knowledge of the God in the face of Jesus Christ." 2 Corinthians 4:6.

"The Bible is food for the soul: "Man shall not live by bread alone, but by every word that proceeds from the mouth of God." Matthew 4:46.

Jesus is the light for the World. "In Him was life, and the life was the light of man." "Then Jesus spoke to them again, saying, I am the light of the world. He who follows me shall not walk-in darkness but have the light of life." John 1:4 and 8:12.

Daily Devotions:

"Genuine success involves doing what the lord has called you to do, not just occasionally but continually. It has to do with persistence rather than perfection. When this is our definition of success, you can know that the Lord wants to succeed." (Dr. Charles Stanley, Sr. Pastor – 1st Baptist Atlanta).

The Major Steps in Processing a Criminal Case:

I was amazed at all the steps taken to process a case regarding criminal acts. They are as follows:

1. Investigation of the rime by the police.

2. Arrest of the suspect by the police

3. Prosecution of a criminal defendant by a district attorney.

4. Indictment by a grand jury or the filling of an information by a prosecutor.

5. Arraignment by a judge.

People Also Ask:

What are the steps in the court process?

What are the 8 steps in a criminal case?

What are the five stages of the criminal justice process?

How many steps are in the criminal justice process?

What six steps occur in a criminal case?

What are the 12 steps of a trial?

What are the 6 steps in a civil case?

What are the 4 stages of a civil case?

What is the process of a court hearing?

What are the steps taken in a felony case?

Do I need a lawyer for a first court appearance?

Who decides if a case goes to trial?

At what stage of the formal criminal justice process does the defendant enter a plea of guilty or not guilty?

What happens in a criminal case?

How long does it take for a prosecutor to file charges?

How long do court hearings last?

Do you go to jail right after a trial?

How long does it take for a criminal case to go to trial?

What happens at a first court appearance?

What is the pretrial process?

How long after being charged does it take to go to court?

What is the criminal procedure law?

What is the order of court proceedings?

How do criminal cases begin?

How do judges decide cases?

What is the court processes?

How does the criminal court work?

What happens at a criminal court hearing?

What court hears criminal cases?

As we may or may not know there are 27 amendments, and I will take you through several of those concerning the subject matter:

1. The 4th amendment protection is for searches and seizures.

2. The 4th amendment states, no warrants for search or arrest.

3. The 5th amendment states, no one can be denied of or deprived of life, liberty or property without due process of the law.

4. The 5th amendment prohibits against double jeopardy trying the same person twice for the same crime if the first trial ended in a conviction of an acquittal.

5. The 6th amendment guaranties a trial by jury, a public trial, confront witnesses, and a right to a lawyer.

6. The 8th amendment prohibits against bails and fines and flames cruel unusual punishment.

CHAPTER 9 -

2020 and Beyond

This is what I noticed in the world today, that good people are the majority. Political and social equality for everyone is a role of ideas made up of governments its not distinction endowed by alienable rights, life, liberty and the pursuit of happiness. The only way to escape is education for everyone. Why does education cost so much because society throughout the world want to establish classes? So, believing in God is our only prescription so far, but ty to become educated now, and just find a way.

Remember God hears you when others do not. My concept in the world we live in, today, is esoteric. Misappropriation all over the place.

Reflection of Life:

This 18th year of the 21st century and violations is punishable by the state and legislatures, it is for the protection of the public. People will learn to hate. Justice and quality are ignored in many homes and countries.

Do not give up on life. You can stifle whatever bitterness you have by operating on a different level, and you will be able to smell the fresh air of freedom, a unique leadership will gregarious, enjoying the company of others. Now you have a complication of life, you will celebrate the energized stadium of life. The fresh air of freedom will incarcerate an understating with a positive outcome and attitude. A societal and liberated, it will reveal a path for observers to duplicate, remain faithful politically and morally for the sake of some observers. They will respect you like you received a noble peace prize. Indicative to what is happening in are world, the essence of your character is immeasurable. How lucky we are that people like Mandela, Obama and Jesus Christ have left a prologue of words and actions show us the way that modern day leadership can be vernacular, can be expressed in all the countries in the world.

The long march of our world's history has eighteen in cities and countries throughout the world – let us keep the momentum going, let us get rid of leaders who put dictators' repulsive ideologies before the rulers of good people of this earth.

On August 23rd, protesters in Hong Kong formed a human chair to show solidarity among the citizens. The chain reached around the city and fell on the anniversary of the Baltic Way. Hong Kong high court has taken action to end these protests, but protestors showed no signs of stopping as the months continue. The calm of the protest was broken as police dispersed tear gas into the crowd.

Protests in Moscow continue; On August 3, the protest as people fought for free and fair elections over 300 people have been arrested thus far, though officials say the number is close to 30.

The epidemic in the Philippines on August 7th; The Philippines declared a national dengue epidemic after 622 people dies between January and July and there were 146,000 cases reported between that time as well.

Taliban bombs Kabul on August 7th; despite peace talks between the Taliban and the U.S., a bomb went off near the police station in Kabul killing 14 people. The Taliban was officially claimed responsibility for the attack. Both sides had previously stated thee was progress during the peace talks, but this displayed a setback.

Mosque shooting in Norway. On August 10th there was a shooting at the Norwegian Mosque injuring at least one person. A suspect was taken into custody and multiple weapons have been found throughout the mosque.

Wedding massacre in Kabul. On August 18th, a suicide bomber entered a wedding in Kabul and blew himself up during the festivities. So far, the death toll was at 63. ISIS has claimed responsibility for the attack.

On August 24, Brazil's leader sent the Army to go fight the fire that had taken hold of the Amazon. President Bolsonaro's decision came after many countries threatened to attack Brazil's economy if he continued ignoring the fire. Many of the fires were said to have been started deliberately.

Arson attack on Bar in Mexico. On August 28th, twenty-three people dies and thirteen were injured in a bar after an arsonist set the place ablaze. No arrests have been made and police have very little information thus far.

Urbanization of earth and all nations today need to pull themselves together a serious discussion and leave out meaningless concepts. They should hold future consideration that we want our children to follow – and should be guided instructions and a collection of rules and show illustrations of basic patterns to follow for inspired satisfaction to be with others. Let us represent a powerful group of communicators to share with the world's governments for pursuing noble relationships throughout.

Methodology: Let us find common definitions that provide symbolic interaction with the world's leaders and provide education through images, shaping circumstances, and communicating with the world much better. But is it enough? An attempt in this pioneering stage to have government come together for the good of the world.

Some countries have enough atomic weapons that could cause serious damage to the world we live in. But it is time to grow up and get together and stop looking and acting like the forces of evil. This world belongs to everyone. If we took a vote presented by citizens of this world, people would say that things could be better for everyone.

Armageddon means a final battle between the forces of good and evil. Seek righteousness. No need to suffer in silence, the world's population have many faces of color and it should not form restrictions. Remember the time for the resurrection draws near and God will not notice color because He made us all. A fulfillment of this vision has assembled and let us make it clear that the separation of people revealed gathering for the tribulation of mankind.

Despite the snares of the customs, people's strong interests refuge because forbidden sculptures and a modest advancement, some system, in government enslave the idea of individuals' progress in fear of tough advancement that maybe contagious is virtues defects humanism, prospering advancement and achievement not to be complicated into the mysteries of ethnocentrism advancement by the individual by emotional, the nature of individuals, and not by government restriction and not controlled by any government policy.

About our diffused planet and knowledge that the influences in educational in ways previously suspected. A view offered was obtained by images of circumstance, 41 million Americans goes to bed hundred. Why? Education, or lack of it.

I reiterate, if you go to complete a course of action that results your demand to secure a better life.

Again, Armageddon – The score of a battle between the forces of good and evil. That word Armageddon has echoed through years, opportunity for mankind has transformed the removing domination by any nations the days of tribulation of admiration, theocratic is a society run by government is the thing of the past. Why? Because we the people notice how to compare the citizen, it is autonomy. We need free universities like the German nation, neither shall they learn war anymore. A book based on world survival – need to help transform earth forever. It is time all people of all countries to put an end of governments' power who wage war. We call can come to earth the same way; women go through agony to give birth. Why they should not have their children die in stupid wars. We are all children of God, why not act like it?

As shown by parable, the separating of spiritual brothers because of their birth locations is bad judgement.

Abolition of racism is a good way to rid the world of unquestioned image of the world today. It is a fact that allegories of social behavior the demands of what God wants it not meant for all of us.

Pattern of life to secure an audience that a religious mindset to influence people all over the world, it this okay. Now let us talk! Journey into lots of countries is not safe. Why is literature not expressing the obstacles? It is because the social values of this not met as it applies far- reaching to people who are easier pray if the family has no finances? The far-reaching concept of that conclusion is discrimination. Let instructors make more money by sharing their skills of knowledge. Some without education commit obvious crimes to survive and some educated commit covert crimes.

Theorizing about democratic countries: Democratic only theories articles written by American civilizations is shaped by the magnitude thrower of are denial of modern-day achievements in education is not available if you are poor.

Surviving the slacken of poor people not getting an increase in verbalized comments it might reflect a slowing down of crime to make higher learning free, by inspiring people with distinctions of positive attitudes about derivatives is the rate of change. The idea of equality, a good example is that all people are equal. The practical situations. This statement true if we are only speaking about futures. We are over-looking demographics. A better word is euphemism or malevolent. I vigorously assert that equality belonging to everyone, remember, God made every race with a distinguishing reflection of what he looks like.

ABOLITIONISM:

While the world is (wavering), abominable, distasteful, thoroughly unpleasant, racism in the United States is happening. Are we really closing doors on people because of their race? The descriptive concern is obviously noticed by adoptive values of the past. Human sensibility adjustment and lack to accommodate repeats itself. Conception by Christian trustworthiness should reveal the practical to reflect the undertaking of what our civilization needs. Not to reject God's creation of what completion of people's approval of superior race. The measure of strength is the capacity for containing contradiction. Opposites can be defined by what we do, rather than what he does. Competitiveness is less dangerous than to extends the conception of a falsehood, practical because on the world stage attitudes developing tribulations.

The effective communication with God is key ingredients to live forever on Earth and in Heaven:

1. Then Jesus again spoke to them saying, "I am the light of the world; he who follows me will not walk in the darkness but will have the light of life."

2. For the bread of God is that which comes down out of Heaven and gives life to the world.

3. He who speaks from himself seeks his own glory; but he who is seeking the glory of the One who sent Him, He is the truth and there is no unrighteousness in Him.

4. While I am in the world, I am the light of the world.

5. Those who will walk by peace and mercy be upon the grace of God may Christ by with spirit and may the grace of our spirit be eternal.

6. If we live by the Spirit let us also walk by the Spirit, let us not become boastful challenging one another and envying one another.

7. I pray that the eyes of your heart may be enlightened, so that you will know what the hope of His calling is, what are the riches of the glory of His inheritance in the saints.

8. Now that no one is justified by the law before God is evident for the righteous man shall live by faith.

9. God is spirit and those who worship Him must worship Him must worship in the spirit and truth.

My message by each year of my life communicating with God:

1. My life communicating with God align some central principles and guidelines, the following is like physical fitness. Some established routines that create mental aspects and to recognize immediate designed that reaches outside remedies of principle disagreements of dominant features outside the vision of society and degradation.

2. The elimination of dialogue and institutional forms that features the elite are a changeable condition. I am convinced social values, a system assessment to eliminate the various issues that contemporary status of a great idea should be shared by everyone such as free schooling, a projection of examining that should be refuted. The idea that you should pay a ton of money for an education, this country should sober up. The imperialism or is a fact to pass off what is good for America to be ordained to create a strong impression that is impracticable and to list as a way of life, less a presentation as successful communication to race around the panic grips to race forward with a reputation is free for everyone, needs immediate attention with adequate preparation for free education finally.

As to fasten together equal compact, a question and answers to infuse the idea that learning, a free leaning process, far exceeds a distinguished way of fairness. Like walking in Faith. Who are poor and White? Is it a separate entity, a periphery a boundary line? We need an increased awareness to be applied for those who are poor. A complete guide of what the future will bring, a guide worth a complete illustration associated with the values of an education regardless.

The distinguished person with an inquisitive mind in America today considers the facts that in observant circle of knowledge 99% believe tuition fees are extreme.

Conclusion: College prices emphasizes, the presentation of a central message, is the elimination of tuition costs period. I come to realization that education is the only way to man kind's problems - a progressive movement – a financial support makes it easy for most students.

The entire history of the United States, "where I was born", the defining feature is racism. Now at a gradual pace is changing for the better. White and Black people have come to realize that influences of change is a necessity, in fact a standard of judgmental views have been measured. For example, never in my life, did I expect to see a black governor in Massachusetts and to witness a Black President who served two terms. My central message is the color of you skin is no longer a central message, is no longer a conclusion to reiterate, that only Caucasians can only be president. Now the door is open for effective leadership regardless of your sex or your complexion. It is no longer a divided society. The differences are specific values, the differences in opinion, from the beginning of history opportunities achieving that carrying forward – innovation.

The process of a new method for early education are to me is an advantage. We as parents, are not to deprive a child from a long-term education. Do not create a disadvantaged child into this world regardless of being Black or poor White. If you are at the age to participate, fine, but made sure a preventative measure is applied.

Early education makes a difference. The entrance of school for some is difficult. Mental nurturing of intelligence is structured by early intellectual stimulation. This is an advantage and beneficial effects for those who are rich.

My increased intensity message is for poor Black and poor white kids. I believe that the departures from school is a socioeconomic mistake. Some thinking is distorted by loved ones who never finish high school therefore statements becoming increasingly structured as a fallacy. An accelerating development in education is a must today, be it sufficiently aware to observe the direction this world is going in educational opportunity will continue to make you and family content to a degree.

FITNESS:

Fitness – being in a condition of being fit, suitability, appropriateness, healthiness, etc. A form, a mood, a 15-minute workout, staring the very first day and make that commitment for one month and then increase to one half hour a day. This procedure will introduce one to a body change, at this point of your training procedure, you would develop a consistent fitness program.

Kick your fitness program into gear by what motivates you, give your mental outlook, people who take on positive outlook are more often receive flattering comments about their accomplishment body-wise.

Now you are at the intersection of innovation of your life. The connector is no longer glimmers of hope but a gateway to a longer healthy life. An inspection of life is in your running will set you free. The drive is like a diesel. You can create a running body that will keep you in good health for years.

BIOLOGY

Energy and Life:

All living things require a continuous source of energy. This energy is used in growth, movement, reproduction and many other activities. There are certain physical laws that describe how energy changes – occur probably the most important rule is that during the process of converting energy from one from to another, some useful energy is lost as useless heat energy. This is known as the second law of thermodynamics. Many of the world's problems result from humans failing to recognize the limits imposed by the laws of thermodynamics. The purpose of this chapter is to show how energy is used and converted within groups of interacting organisms and how the laws of thermodynamics apply in living systems.

Ecology and environment:

Today many people use the "in works" ecology and environment. Students, housewives, politicians, various types of planners and union leaders speak of environmental issues. Although the words are commonly used, they are often used, incorrectly or slanted in meaning toward the speaker's particular point of view.

Ecology is nothing more than the study of organisms as in relationship to their environment. This is a simple definition for an overly complex study. Both living and non-living factions play a part in the environment of any organism.

When anglers decide on which bait to use, they are dealing with a living part of the environment. The temperature of the water is a non-living factor in the life of a fish. In any ecological study, a vast number of living and non-living factors must be considered.

What is an ecologist? Does one need a college degree to become an ecologist? We are all ecologists in one form or another. If you are an angler. Your goal is to catch fish. The more you know about fish and their relationship to their environment, the most successful you will be at catching them. We are all interested in the relationship of organisms to their environment, even if the only organism we are concerned about is ourselves.

The environment is overly complex. Therefore, the study of any organism's environment is extraordinarily complex. A plant is influenced by many different factors during its lifetime – the type and amount of minerals in the soil. The amount of sunlight hitting the plant, the animals that eat plants, and the wind, water, and temperatures. Each item in this list can be further divided into other areas of study. For instance, water is important in the life of plants and so rainfall. A study of plant ecology not just how much rain, but the time of the year the rain falls. Is it a hard driving rain or a soft gentle rain? Does the water soak into the ground for later use, or does it quickly run off into the rivers? Is it a warm or cold rain? Though rain fall seems to be an easily understood portion of an ecological study, it is really an overly complex subject.

Temperature is another subject that is important in the life of a plant. For example, two areas of the world can have the same average daily temperature as well – 10 degree C but not have the same plants because of different temperature extremes. In one area of temperature maybe 13 degree C in the say and 7 degree C at night. For a 10 degree C average. In another area, the temperature may be 20 degree C in the day and 0 degree C at night. For a 10 degree C average plants react to extremes in temperatures as well as to the average. Temperatures may influence only certain parts of a plant. The tomato plant will grow at a temperature below 13 degree C but will not set fruit at that temperature. The animals in an area are influenced as much as nonliving factors do not favor the growth of plants, there will be little food and few hiding places for the animal life. Two types of areas that support only a small animal biomass are polar regions and deserts near the polar regions of the earth. The temperature inhibits plant growth. As a result, these areas have relatively few species of animals and these animals have small populations. Desserts receive little rainfall and so have poor plant growth and low animal biomass. On the other hand, tropical rain forest has excellent plant growth and a high animal biomass.

Living organisms themselves are a vital part of any environment. If there are too many animals in an area, they could demand such large amounts of food that all plant life would be destroyed and the animals themselves would die. In the human population, living parts of the environment include the family, co-workers, fellow students, the neighborhood mugger and the other guy. They all have an influence on your life. Please do not forget the fly on the table, the bacteria in your food, the rat in the sewer, the shade tree in the yard and the barking dog next door. These are only a few examples of the many living things that are a part of your environment.

Because of transportation and social and political ties, humans have the whole world as their environment. Our cotton may come from Texas, your oranges from Florida your lettuce from California, your camera from Japan, your copper from Chile and your oil from Saudi Arabia. If hundreds of acres of orange groves in Florida are destroyed to make way for an amusement area, there may be certain local economic rewards. But that area no longer produces oranges, which might change the price of oranges for Midwesterners. As another example, the government of Chile decided to process cooper within its own country to raise the standard of living of the native people, this was good for their environment, but now the price of copper has increased. How does that effect the cost of building a house in the United States? The cost of electric wiring and copper plumbing has risen and therefore a house costs more to build.

Surely your environment and that of all other people in the world is an overly complex one. Before you decide that something is good or bad for the environment, step back and view the whole picture. Look at all aspects of everyone's environments since changes will influence some part of the environment, either now or in the future. Lumbering, for example, has environment, now or in the future. Lumbering has affected many good trout streams. The trees next to the stream provided shade and kept the water cool enough to maintain a healthy trout population. Once the trees were removed, the water temperature rose to a point at which trout could no longer survive.

One of the most important things influencing any population is the amount of available energy. Since energy for living organisms is captured by green plants, they determine the kinds and numbers of different populations in an area.

The Organization of Living Systems:

Green plants play the role of an organism is called its niche. The niche of the green plant to capture sunlight to manufacture sugar. In ecological terms, green plants referred to as producers. Producers convert inorganic material into organic material. The energy that plants trap can be transferred through several other organisms before it is completely lost to the environment as useless heat energy. Each time the energy enters a different organism it is said to enter a different trophic level or state of energy flow.

The plants receive the energy directly from the sun and they occupy the first trophic level. All animals are consumed but occupy different trophic levels depending on whether they receive their energy directly or indirectly from the plants. Those animals that feed directly on plants are caller herbivores and occupy the second trophic level. Those that feed on other animals are called carnivores and occupy the third trophic level. Organisms that receive their energy from eating carnivores occupy even higher trophic levels. For example, a man may eat a fish that ate a frog, that ate spiders, that ate on insect that relied on plants for food, in this example, there are six trophic levels. Some animals do not fall neatly into either category but are both carnivores and herbivores. These are call omnivores. Their trophic level is not easy to identify.

If a plant or animal dies, the energy within its body is finally released to the environment as heat by organisms that decompose the body into its most basic molecules, such as carbon dioxide and water. These organisms of decay are called decomposers. Organisms such as bacteria and fungi occupy this last of the trophic levels. This reprocessing is the oldest and most effective form of recycles. If the sun provides the necessary energy, elements are recycling over and over again. This process is almost as old as life on the earth and is essential if life is to continue.

Note: "Ecology and environment and Energy and Life" (The Third Edition by: Eldon D. Enger, Andrew H. Gibson, Richard Kormelink, Frederick C. Ross and Rodney J. Smith).

Your description, explanation and interpretation, theories and a sprinkling of humor and accuracy was right on!!

CHAPTER 10

The Most Influential African-American Leaders and Inventors in U.S. History

The individuals listed here were before my time on earth and/or present today:

1. President Barack H. Obama – 45th President of the United States – the first Black American to be elected (twice) into the highest office of the Nation.

2. Reverend Jesse L. Jackson – A pastor and civil rights activist

3. Reverend Al Sharpton – A pastor and civil rights activist. A commentator on the TV news program MSNBC; and president of National Action Network.

4. Retired General Colin Powell. An American politician, diplomat and a retired 4-star general who served in the Army. He was the 65th Secretary of State from 2001-2005.

5. Harriet Tubman – Escaped slavery to become a leading abolitionist and political activist. She led hundreds of enslaved people to freedom along the route of the Underground Railroad.

6. Rosa Parks – A civil rights activists who refused to surrender her seat to a White passenger on a segregated bus in Montgomery, Alabama.

It sparked to highly publicized Montgomery Bus Boycott. The U.S. Congress has called her "the first lady of civil rights" and the "Mother of the freedom movement."

7. Ida B. Wells – An investigative journalist, educator and an early leader in the civil rights' movement. She was one of the founders of the National Association for the Advancement of Colored People (NAACP)

8. Ella Josephine Baker – A civil rights and human rights activist. She worked alongside some of the most noted civil rights leaders of the 20th century including W.E.D. DuBois, Thurgood Marshal and Martin Luther King.

9. Majora Carter – American urban revitalization strategist and public radio host from the South Bronx area of New York City. Carter founded and led the non-profit Environmental Justice Solution Corporation "Sustainable South Bronx."

10. Mark Anthony Neal – An author and academic. He is Professor of Black Popular Culture in the Department of African and African-American Studies at Duke University where he won the 2010 Robert B. Cox Award for Teaching.

11. Roy Emile Alfredo Innis – An activists and politician. He was National Chairman of the Congress of Racial Equality (CORE) from 1968 until his death. One of his son's Niger Roy Innis serves ad National Spokesman of the congress of Racial Equality.

12. Lonnie Isabel – Reporter, Editor and Journalism instructor who has covered U.S. politics and foreign affairs for three decades. He led coverage of 9/11, Iraq War and several presidential campaigns. He teaches at Columbia University Graduate School of Journalism.

13. Nina Gamble Kennedy (born 1960) is a classical pianist, orchestral conductor, film maker and writer.

14. Darlene Clark Hine – An author and professor. She is known for her expertise in the field of African-American history. She is a recipient of the National Humanities Medal.

15. William Jalani Cobb – A writer, author and educator. The Ira A. Lipman Professor of Journalism of Columbia University, Cobb was previously an associate professor of history and director of the institute for American-American studies at the University of Connecticut in Storrs, Conn. From 2012-2016.

16. Paula Giddings – A writer and an African-American historian. She is the author of "When And Where I entice the Impact of Black Women on Race And Sex In America", "In Search Of sisterhood: Delta Sigma Theta and "The Challenge of the Black Sorority Movement and "Ida: A Sword Among Lions."

17. Baker Kitwana – Former editor-in-chief of the Source Magazine where he wrote and edited hundreds of articles on hip-hop, youth culture, politics and national affairs.

18. Joshua Guild – He specializes in twentieth Century African-American social and cultural history, urban history and the making of the modern African diaspora with particular interests in migration, Black internationalism, Black popular music and the Black radical tradition. A graduate of Wesleyan University where he was a Mellon Mays Undergraduate Fellow, he received his PhD in history and African American Studies from Yale.

19. Khalil Gibran Muhammad – Is a professor of History, Race and Public Policy at Harvard Kennedy School and the Suzanne Young Murray professor at the Radcliffe Institute for Advanced Studies.

20. March Hayden Morial – A political and civic leader and the current president of the National Urban League. Morial served as Mayor of New Orleans from 1994-2002, President of the United States Conference of Mayors in 2001 and Louisiana State Senate from 1991-1994.

21. Shirley Sherrod – Is a former Georgia State Director of Rural Development for the United States Department of Agriculture. On July 19, 2010, she became a subject of controversy when parts of a speech she gave were publicized by Breitbart News and she was forced to resign.

22. James Young – A professional basketball player of Maccabi Haifa of the Israeli Premier League. He played one season of college basket-

ball for the Kentucky Wildcats before being selected with the 17th overall pick in the 2014 NBA draft by the Boston Celtics.

23. George E. Curry – An journalist. Considered the "dean of Black press columnists", Curry's weekly commentaries enjoyed wide syndication for Sports Illustrated, he died of heart failure August 20th, 2016. Earlier in his career he worked for St. Louis Post-Dispatch, and Chicago Tribune.

24. Beverly "Bevy" Smith – Is a television personality and businesswoman. She is best known for her work as a co-host on BRAVO's fashion-themed talk show Fashion Queens.

25. Clarence Lusane – Is an author, activist, lecturer and freelance journalist. His most recent major work is his book, "The Black History of the White House." Other books written by Lusane include "Hitler's Black Victims", Colin Powell and Condolessa Rice", "Race in the Global Era", and "No Easy Victories: Black American and the Vote."

26. Obery M. Hendricks Jr. – Is a visiting research scholar at Columbia University. Before taking this position, he was a professor at Drew University and a visiting professor at Princeton Theological Seminary. He has also served as president of Payne Theological Seminary, the oldest African-American theological institutions.

27. Mary Wilson – Singer. She is a vocalist, concert performer, music rights activists, motivational speaker, author and former U.S. Cultural Ambassador. She was part of the Supremes music group. (Before finishing my book, Ms. Wilson died in Las Vegas, Nevada on February 8, 2021).

28. Lonnie Bunch III – Is an educator and historian. Bunch is the 14th Secretary of the Smithsonian Institute, the first African-American and first historian to serve as head of the Smithsonian. He has spent most of his career as a history museum curator and administrator.

29. Robin D.G. Kelley – A historian and academic, who is the Gary B. Nash Professor of American History at UCLA. From 2006 to 2011, he was professor of American Studies and Ethnicity at the University of Southern California.

30. Peniel E. Joseph – A scholar, teacher and leading public voice on race issues who holds a joint professorship appointment at the LBJ School of Public Affairs and the History Department in the College of Liberal Arts at the University of Texas at Austin.

31. Harris Perry – Associate professor of Politics and African-American Studies at Princeton University. Also, a contributor at MSNBC (TV News Station).

32. Marcus Garvey Jr. – was a Jamaican political activist, publisher, journalist, entrepreneur and orator. He was the founder and first President General of the Universal Negro Improvement Association and African Communities League, through which he declared himself provisional President of Africa. He led the "back to Africa movement."

33. Nelson Mandela – Was a South African anti-apartheid revolutionary, political leader and philanthropist who served as President of South Africa from 1994-1999. He was the country's first official elected in a fully representative democratic election.

34. Lewis Howard Latimer – Pioneer of the electric lighting system. His name will be forever associated with two of the most revolutionary inventions of all time, the incandescent electric light bulb and the telephone.

35. Jan Ernst Matzeliger – Invented the automatic shoe lasting machine, mechanizing the complex process of joining a shoe sole to its upper and revolutionizing the shoe industry. Matzeliger was born in Dutch Guiana and was self-educated.

36. Elija McCoy – 19th Century inventor of the automatic lubricating devices. He invented lubrication devices used to make train travel more efficient. He is the "Real McCoy"…as the saying goes.

37. Norbert Rillieux – American-French inventor born in New Orleans, LA., was widely considered one of the earliest chemical engineers. He revolutionized sugar processing. His pioneering invention of the multiple-effect evaporator which was an important development in the growth of the sugar industry.

38. Grandville T. Woods – Was an inventor who held more than 60 patents in the U.S. He was the first African-American mechanical and electrical engineer after the Civil War. Self-taught, he concentrated most of his work on trains and streetcars.

39. Garrett A. Morgan – The country's most successful inventor, created two – the gas mask and the three position traffic signal.

40. Frederick McKinley Jones – An inventor (multi-racial [White father and Black mother]) invented the refrigeration for trucks – the long-haul transporters. He co-founded Thermo King Company.

41. Dr. George Carruthers – A scientist, he invented the ultraviolet camera, spectrograph for NASA to use when it launched Apollo 16 in 1972. Is work also demonstrated the molecular hydrogen exists in the interstellar medium.

42. Kamala Harris – Recently elected Vice President is the first woman and first woman of color to hold this position. Before the election, she was the Jr. U.S. Senator from California. Her earlier position was as an Attorney General for California.

There are many more to be recognized, which would mean a separate book altogether. The names listed are a mere sample of all the accomplishments made by Black citizens of our Nation.

IN CONCLUSION

Under magnetic influence, I appreciate the 84 years of living as a United States citizen. By the time this book is published, through God Grace, I will be 85. The knowledge that was shared by interacting with people from many backgrounds and ethnic and racial groups is unmeasurable. If God takes my life today, I can say with a clear heart and mind, that I had an exceedingly enjoyable life.

During the time attempting to finish my book, I have personally witnessed the worst and the best in our country. Never in my life, have I experienced the outbreak of a deadly virus sweeping, not just American soil, but countries around the world. Not only are we facing a pandemic, but social and racial injustice and the response to it. We are being torn apart in our Nation. Our very foundation of our democracy and our American ideals are at stake.

If we focus hard enough, we as a people can turn this difficult time into an opportunity. An opportunity to unite and create a society that values hope over hate, faith over fear and compassion over confrontation.

I am in constant prayer for the healing of our country and am hopeful that we combat the Corona Virus, turn our economy around for the better, fix our healthcare system and leave a healthy economic system for our children and grandchildren.

I would love for my book to be in the hands of many to read and enjoy as a learning tool sprinkled with some historical events.

Lastly, but importantly, I want to thank my darling wife, Dorothy Wiggins, for her efforts of encouragement in my attempt to write my first book. May God bless all and please read my book.

REFERENCES

Websites:

Britannica.com/American History/Events

www.Wikipedia.org

www.history.com

www.britannia.com/World History

Bay State Banner, August 3, 2010

"The Call To Teach", Matthew Lynch, Ed.D – editor of the Edvocate

InTouch Ministries, Dr. Reverend Charles Stanley

AARP Magazine – Editorial Section (1/2021)